CHRISTMAS FAVORITES

80 HOLIDAY CLASSICS FOR ORGAN

ISBN 978-1-4950-2004-9

HAL•LEONARD® CORPORATION

7777 W. BLUEMOUND RD. P.O. BOX 13819 MILWAUKEE, WI 53213

Visit Hal Leonard Online at
www.halleonard.com

Angels We Have Heard on High

ation 14

Traditional French Carol
Translated by James Chadwick

oderately

Gmaj7　　G#dim　　　D7　　　　G　　　　　D　　G

An - gels　we　have　heard　on　high,　Sweet - ly　sing - ing

7sus4　D7　G　　Gmaj7　G#dim　　D7　　G　　　D　G

o'er　the plains;　And　the moun - tains　in　re - ply　Ech - o - ing　their

7sus4　G　　　G　　E7　　Am　　D7　　G　　C

y - ous strains.　Glo　-　-　-　-　-
Lower

G　D　G　C　|1 G　　D7　　|2 G　　D7　　G

ri - a　in　ex - cel - sis　De　-　o,　De　-　o.

R.H. to Upper

Ah! Dearest Jesus, Holy Child

Registration 15

Translated by Rev. J. Troutbeck
Harmonized by J.S. Bach

Angels from the Realms of Glo

Registration 2

Words by
Mus

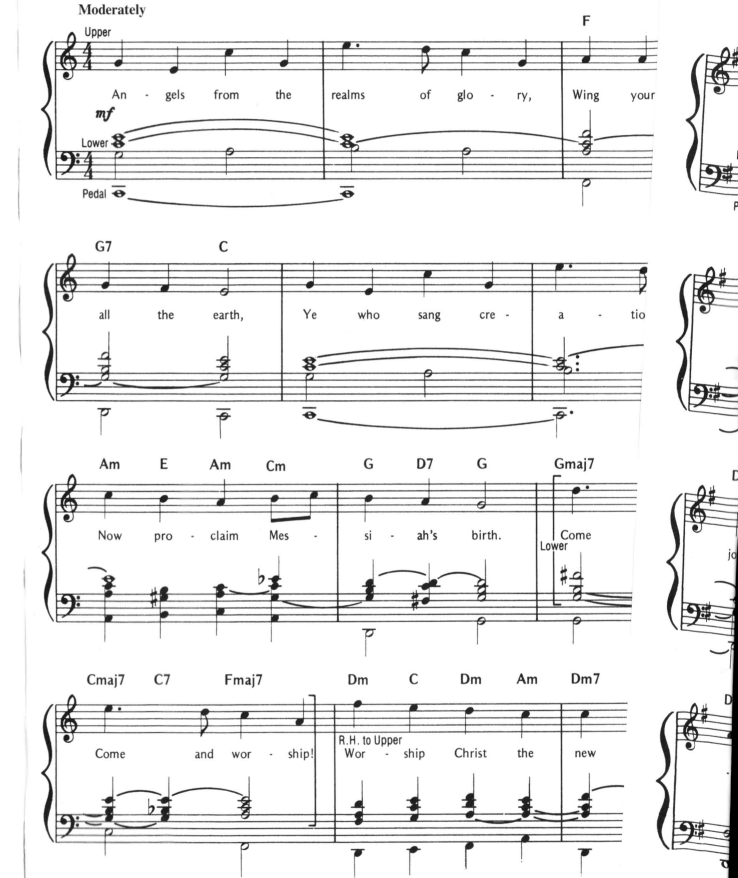

Away in a Manger

Registration 12

Anonymous Text
Music by James R. Murray

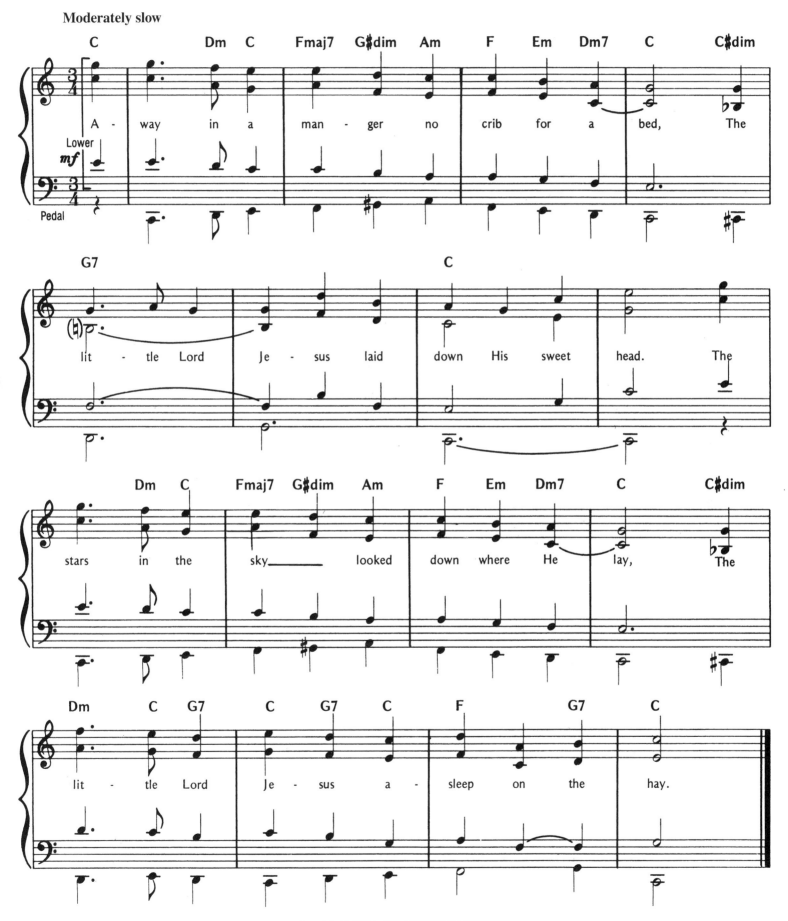

Auld Lang Syne

Registration 7

Words by Robert Burns
Traditional Scottish Melody

Away in a Manger

Registration 1

Anonymous Text
Music by Jonathan E. Spillman

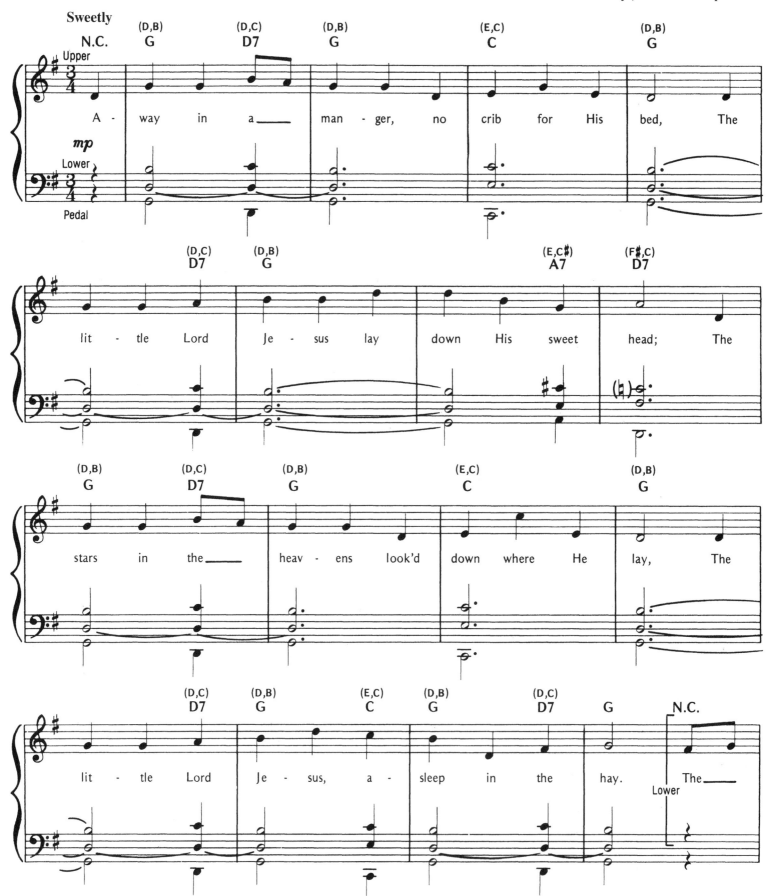

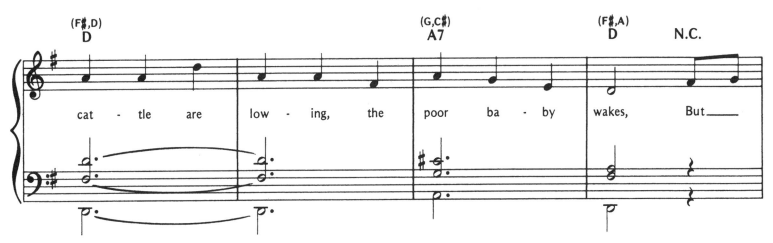

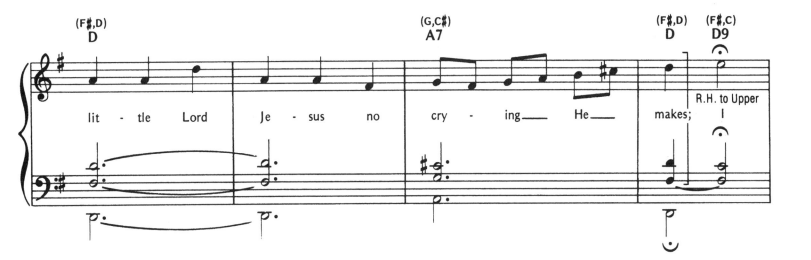

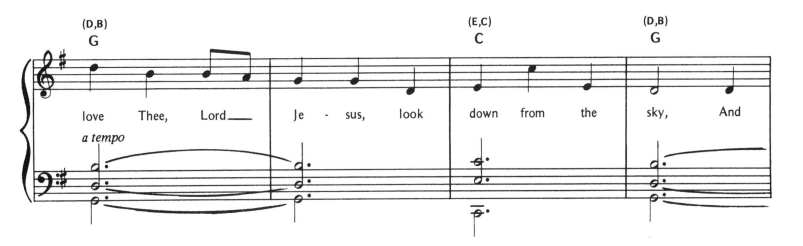

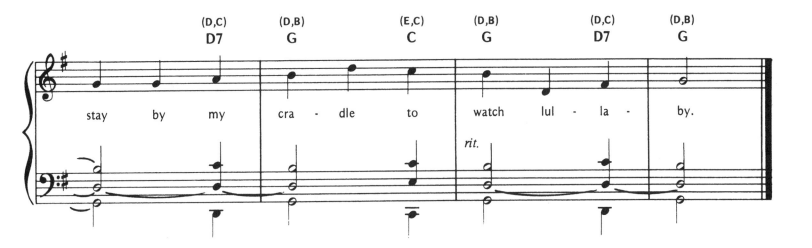

Beside Thy Cradle Here I Stand
from THE CHRISTMAS ORATORIO

Registration 5

Words by Paul Gerhardt
Translated by Rev. J. Troutbeck
Music from *Geistliche Gesangbuch*

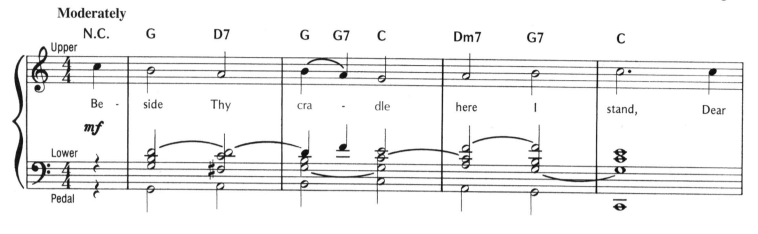

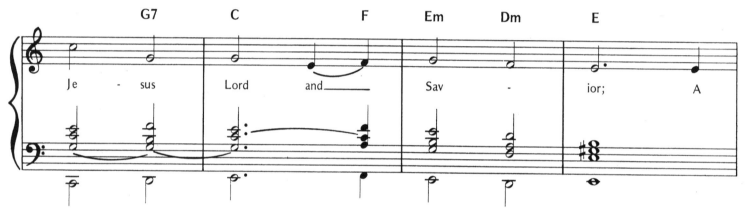

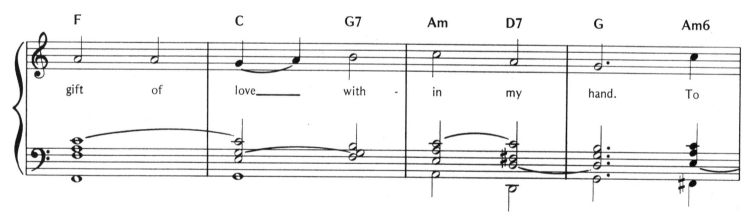

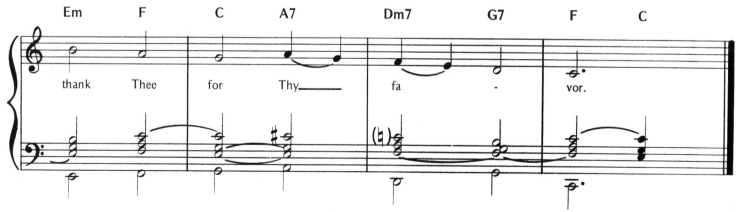

Christ Was Born on Christmas Day

Registration 17

Traditional

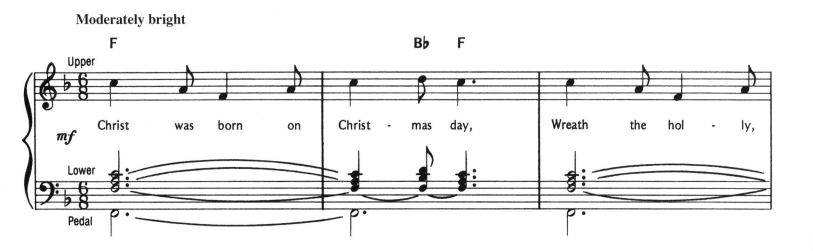

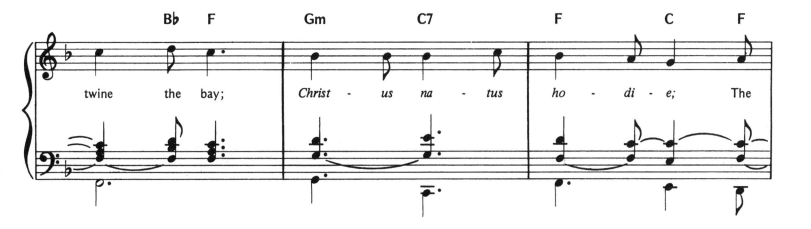

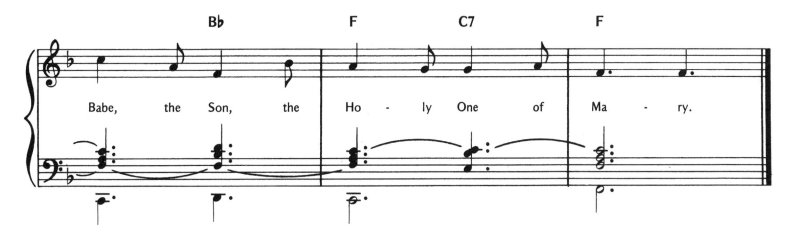

Blue Christmas

Registration 25

Words and Music by Billy Hayes
and Jay Johnson

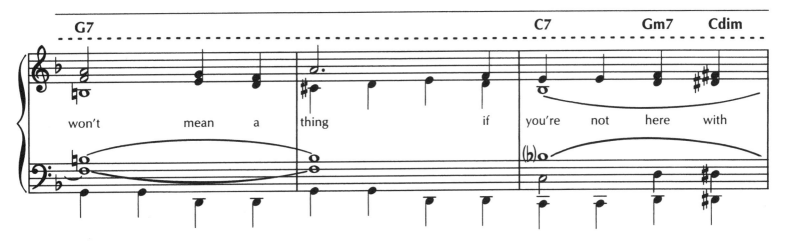

won't mean a thing if you're not here with

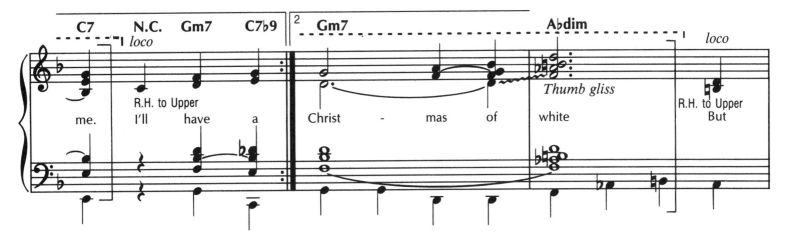

me. I'll have a Christ - mas of white But

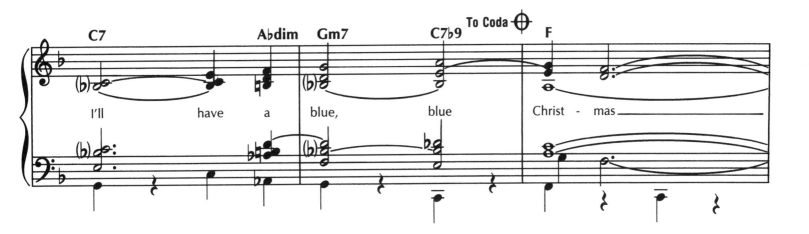

I'll have a blue, blue Christ - mas

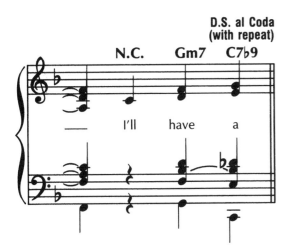

I'll have a

Christ - mas.

The Chipmunk Song

Registration 36

Words and Music by
Ross Bagdasarian

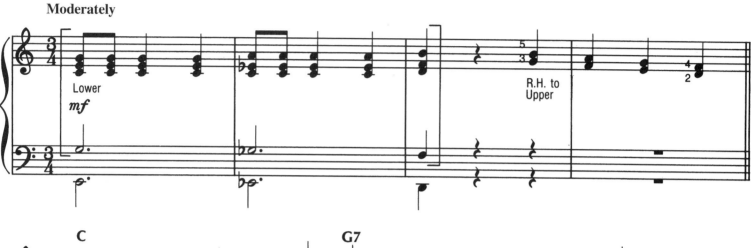

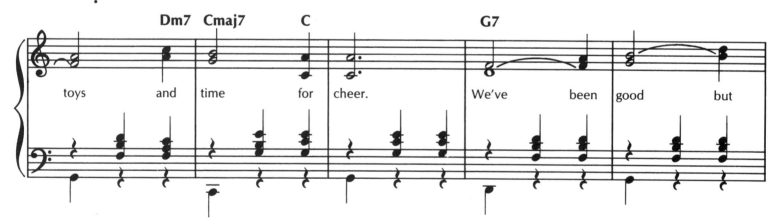

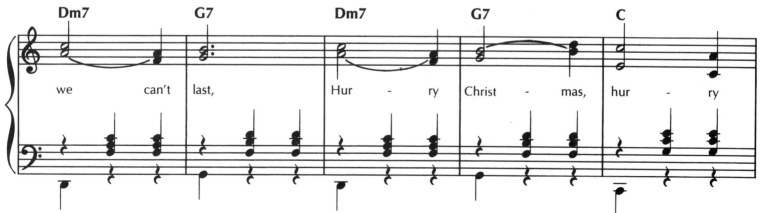

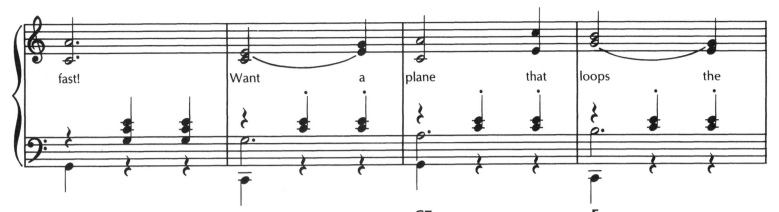

fast!　　Want　　a　plane　that　loops　　the

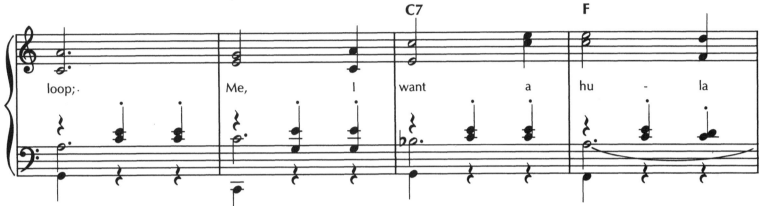

C7　　　　　　　　　　　　　　　　　　**F**

loop;·　　Me,　I·　want　　a　hu　-　la

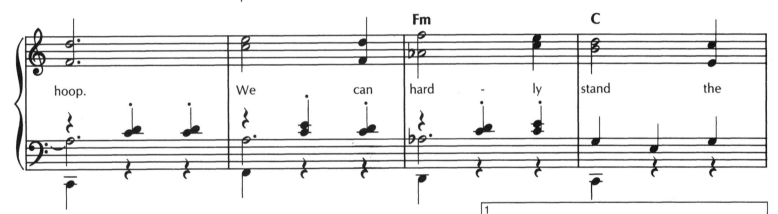

Fm　　　　　　　　　　　**C**

hoop.　　We　can　hard　-　ly　stand　　the

D9　　　**D7**　　**G7**　　　　　　　　　1　　**C**

wait.　　Please　Christ　-　mas　don't　be　late.

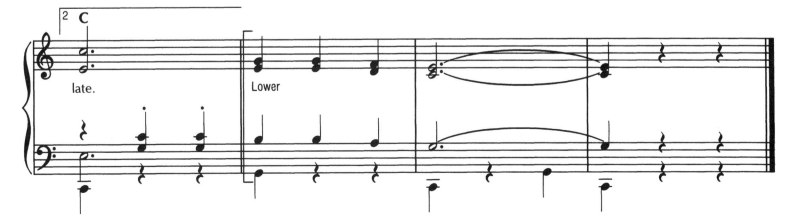

2　**C**

late.　　　Lower

C-H-R-I-S-T-M-A-S

Registration 49

Words by Jenny Lou Carson
Music by Eddy Arnold

Moderately, with expression

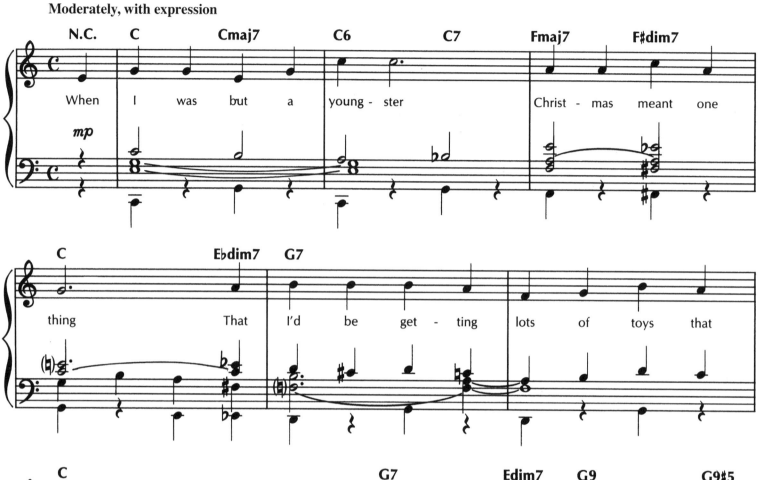

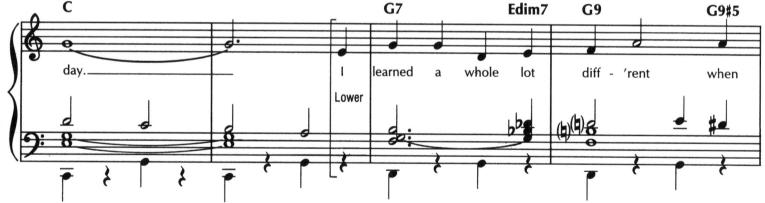

19

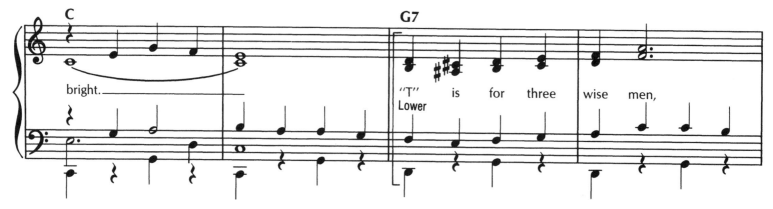

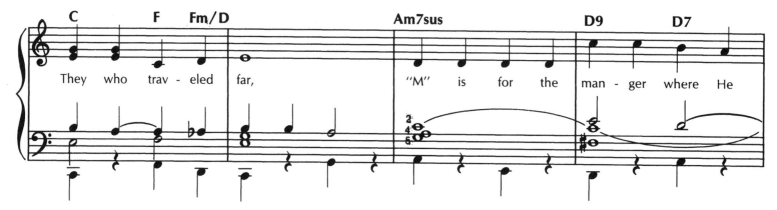

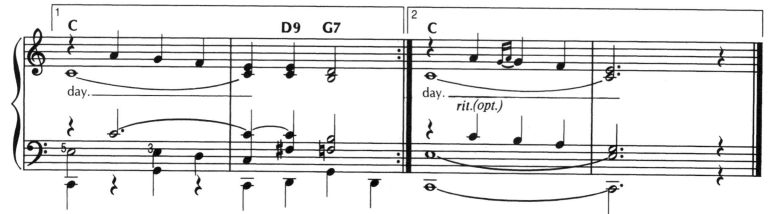

Come, All Ye Shepherds

Registration 13

Traditional Czech Text
Traditional Moravian Melody

Christmas Time Is Here

from A CHARLIE BROWN CHRISTMAS

Registration 25

Words by Lee Mendelson
Music by Vince Guaraldi

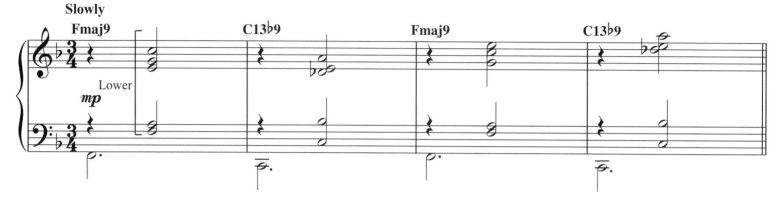

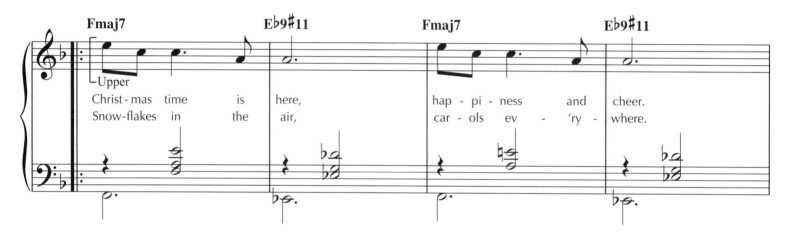

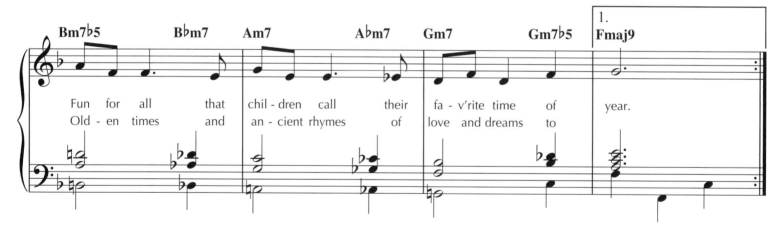

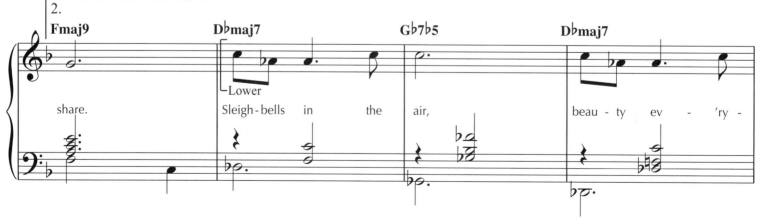

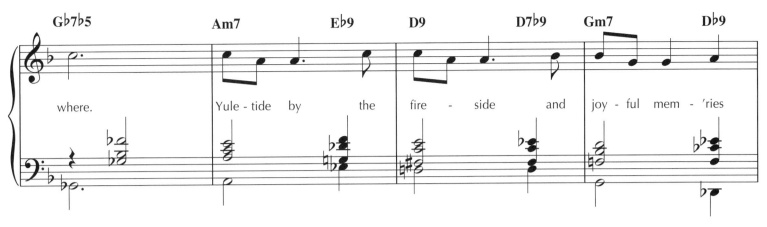

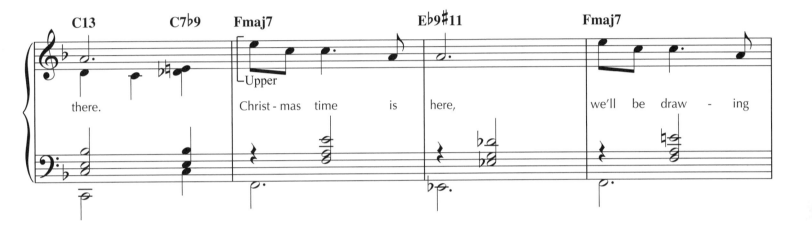

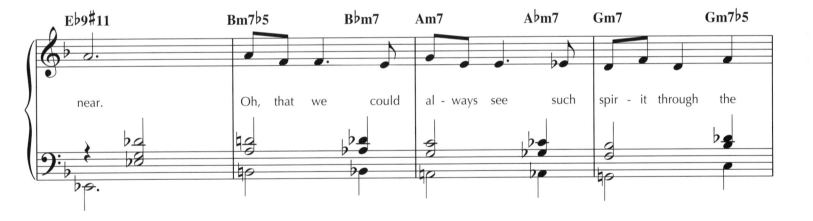

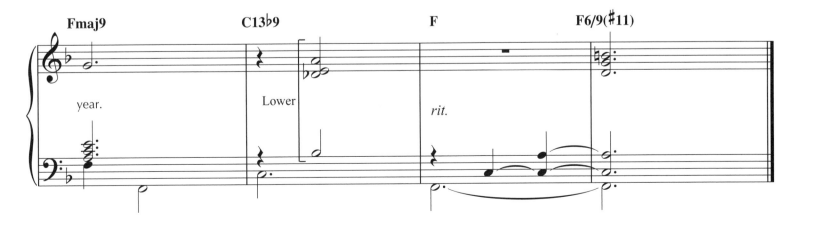

The Christmas Waltz

Registration 51

Words by Sammy Cahn
Music by Jule Styne

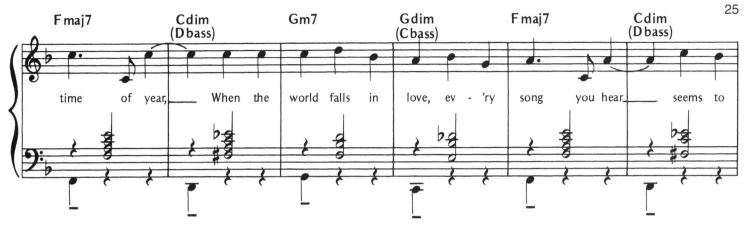

time of year,___ When the world falls in love, ev - 'ry song you hear___ seems to

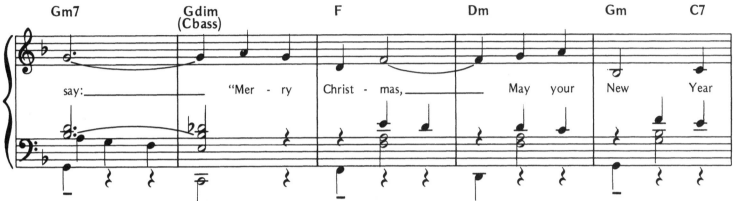

say:___ "Mer - ry Christ - mas,___ May your New Year

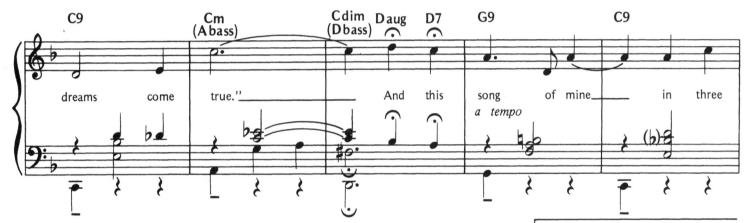

dreams come true."___ And this song of mine___ in three

a tempo

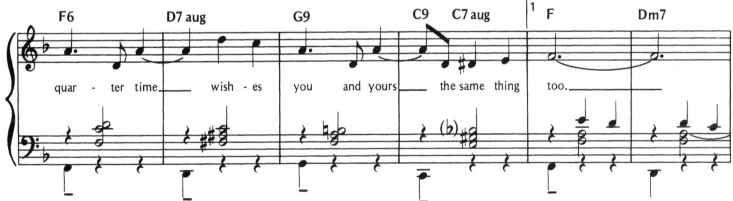

quar - ter time___ wish - es you and yours the same thing too.___

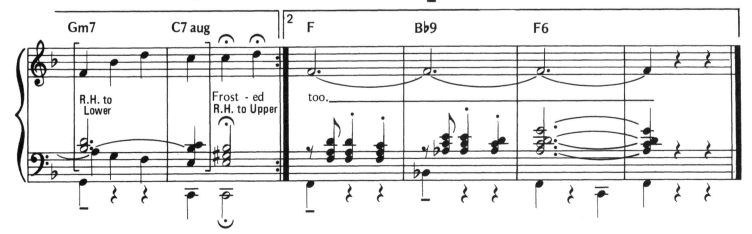

R.H. to Lower

Frost - ed R.H. to Upper

too.___

Coventry Carol

Registration 16

Words by Robert Croo
Traditional English Melody

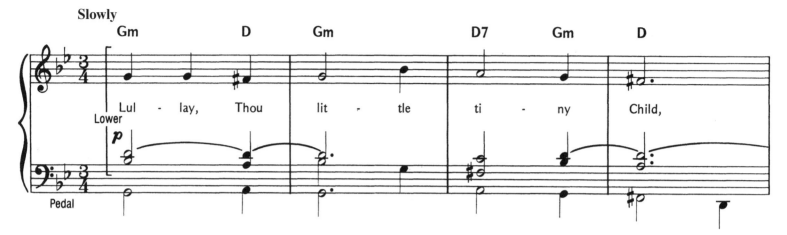

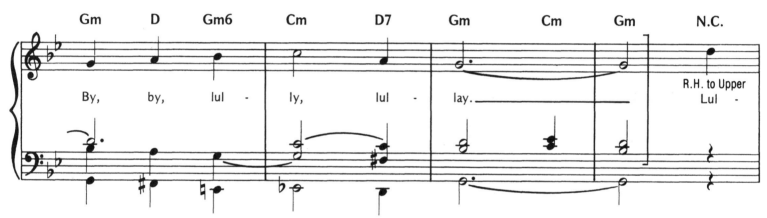

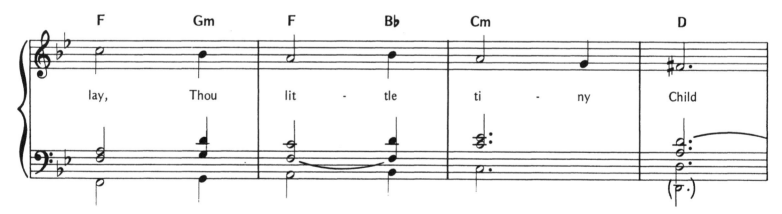

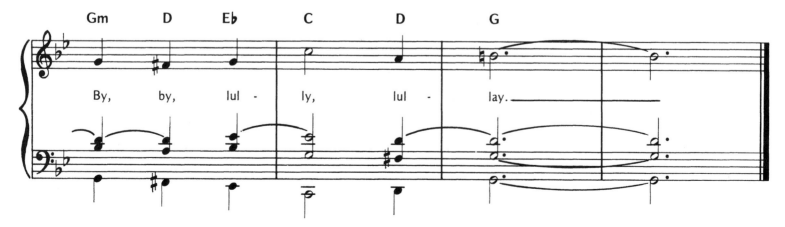

Deck the Hall

Registration 7

Traditional Welsh Carol

Dance of the Sugar Plum Fairy
from THE NUTCRACKER

Registration 3

By Pyotr Il'yich Tchaikovsky

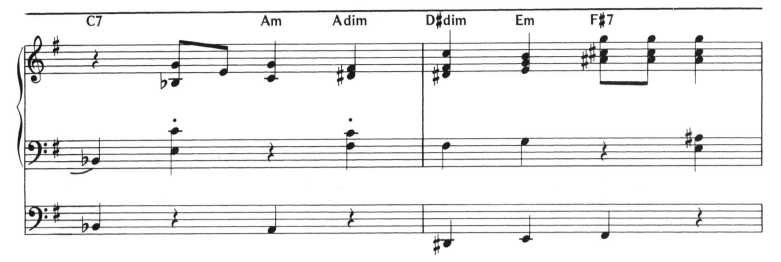

The First Noël

Registration 17

17th Century English Carol
Music from W. Sandys' *Christmas Carols*

The Friendly Beasts

Registration 13

Traditional English Carol

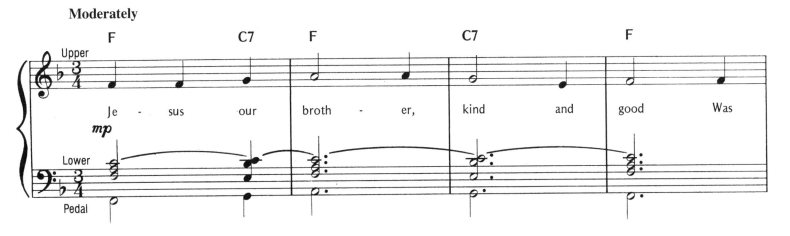

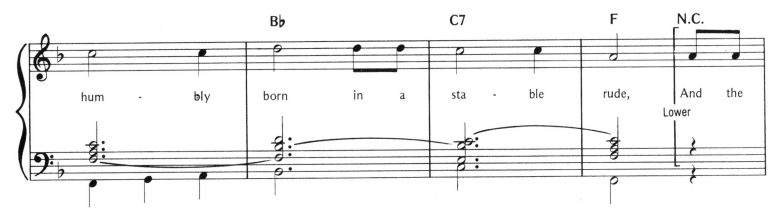

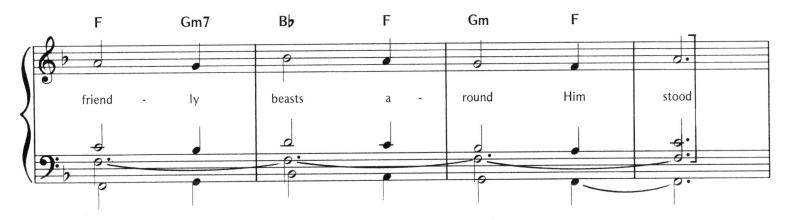

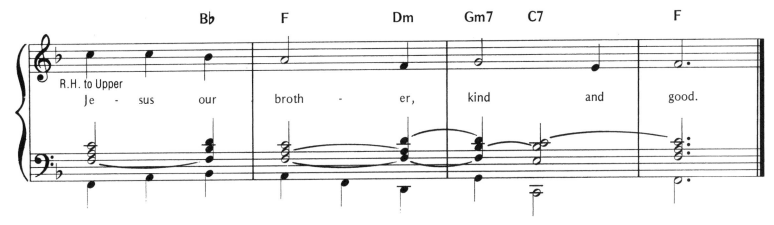

Frosty the Snow Man

Registration 30

Words and Music by Steve Nelson
and Jack Rollins

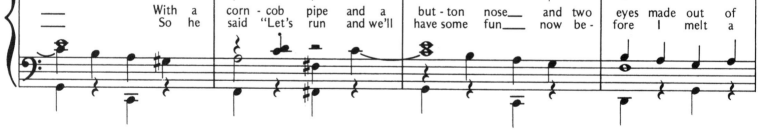

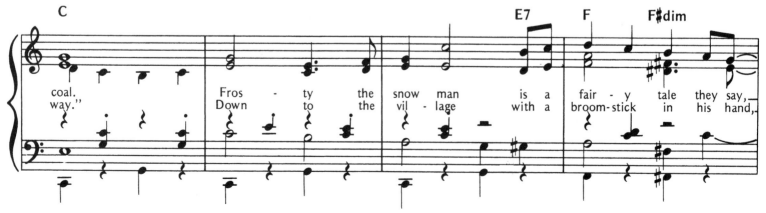

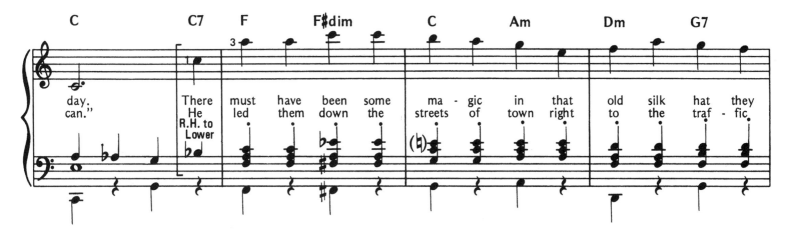

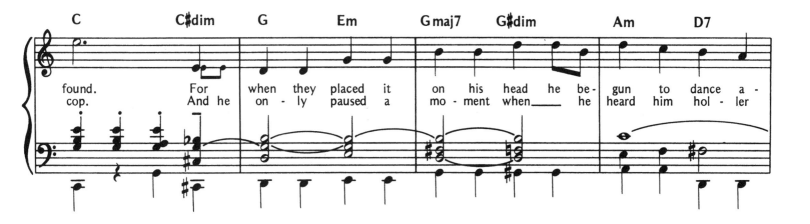

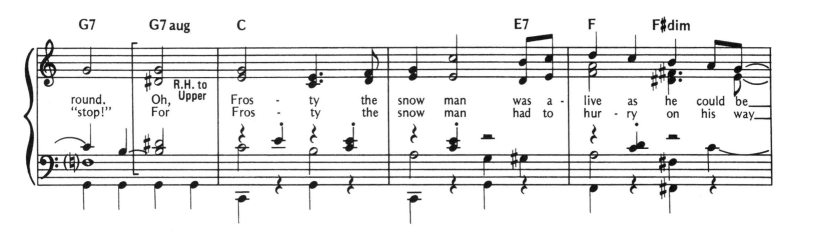

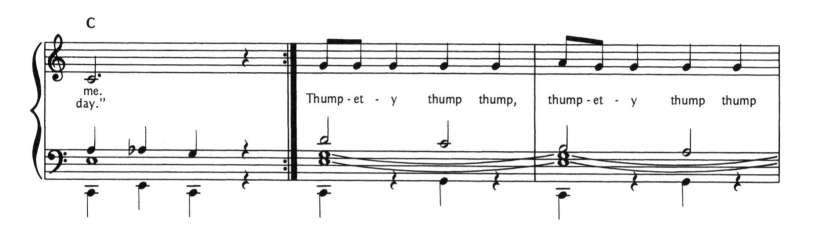

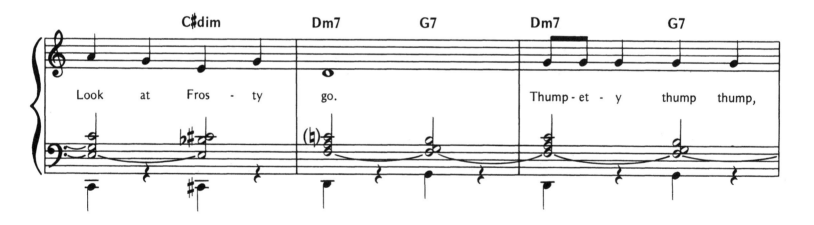

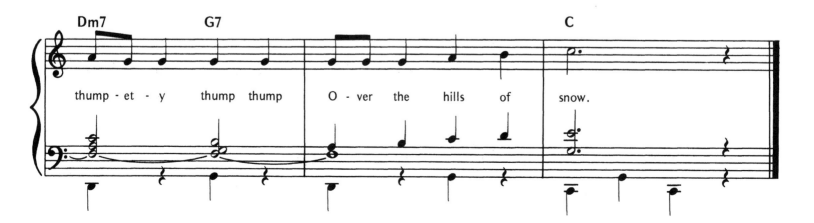

Go, Tell It on the Mountain

Registration 7

African-American Spiritual
Verses by John W. Work, Jr.

God Rest Ye Merry, Gentlemen

Registration 4

19th Century English Carol

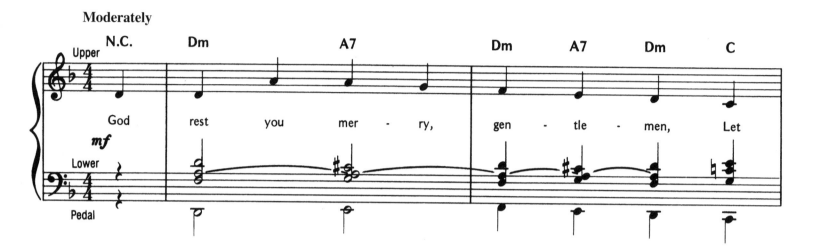

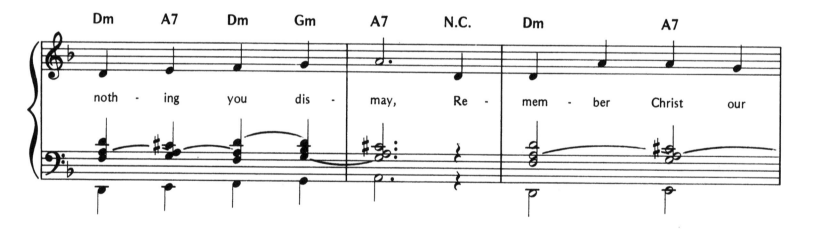

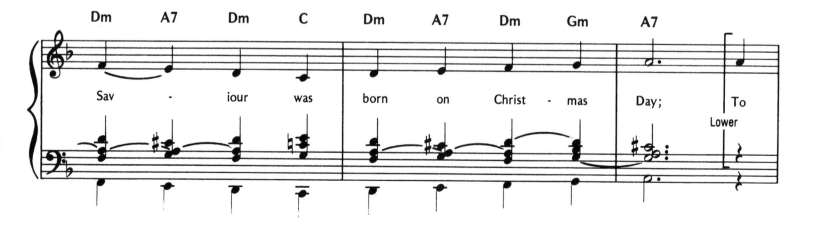

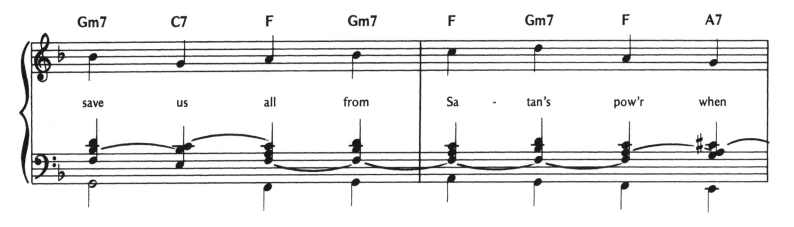

save us all from Sa - tan's pow'r when

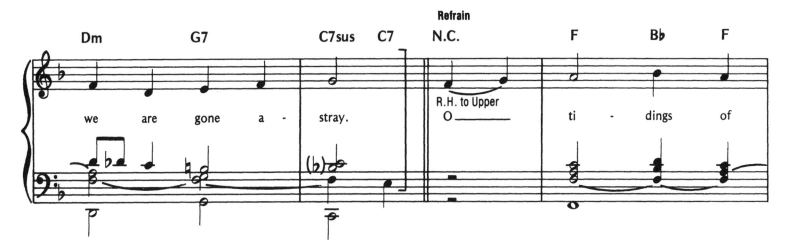

Refrain

we are gone a - stray. O _____ ti - dings of

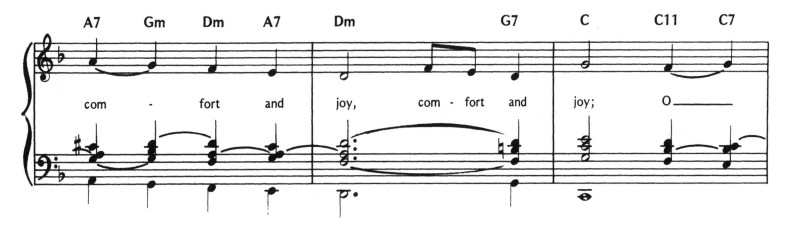

com - fort and joy, com - fort and joy; O _____

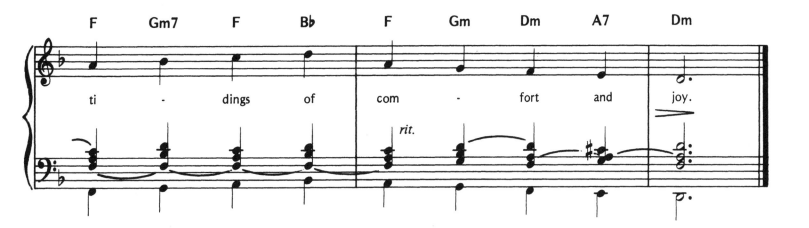

ti - dings of com - fort and joy.

Good Christian Men, Rejoice

Registration 5

14th Century Latin Text
Translated by John Mason Neale
14th Century German Melody

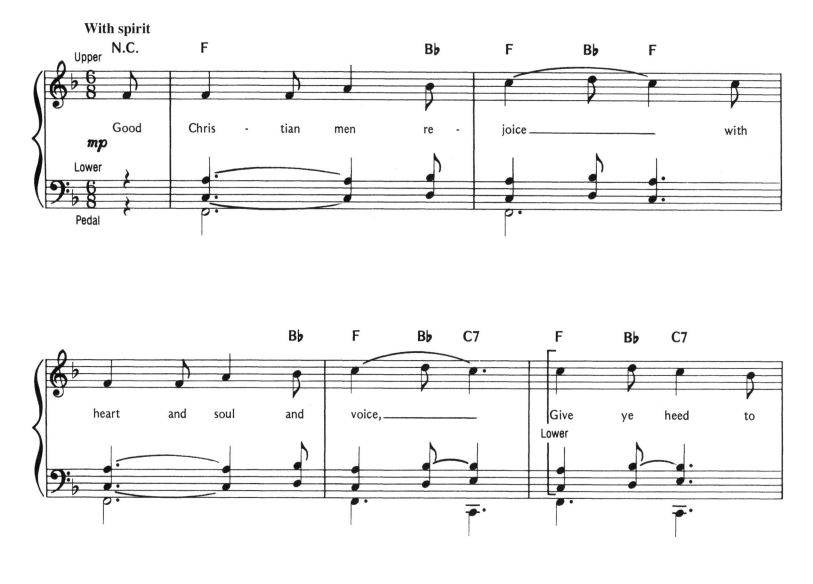

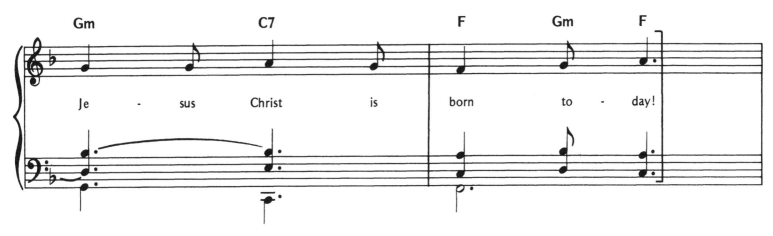

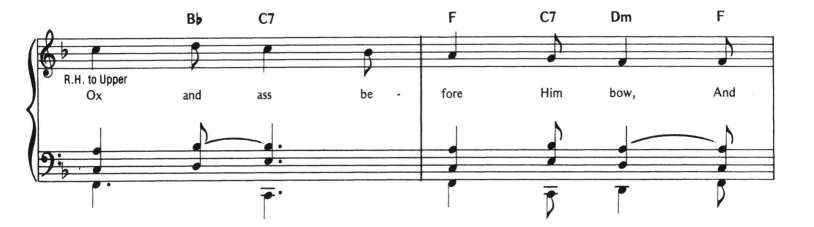

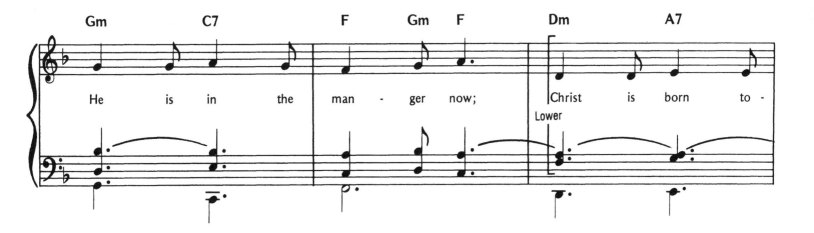

Good King Wenceslas

Registration 7

Words by John M. Neale
Music from *Piae Cantiones*

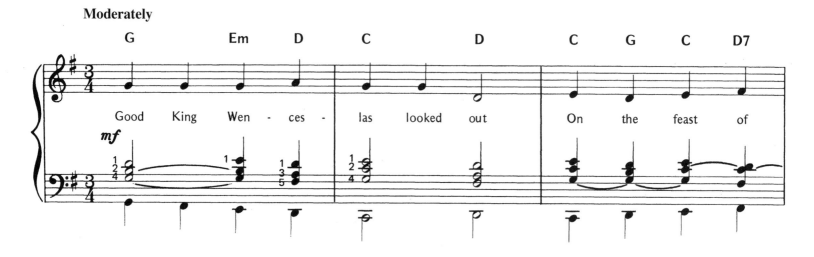

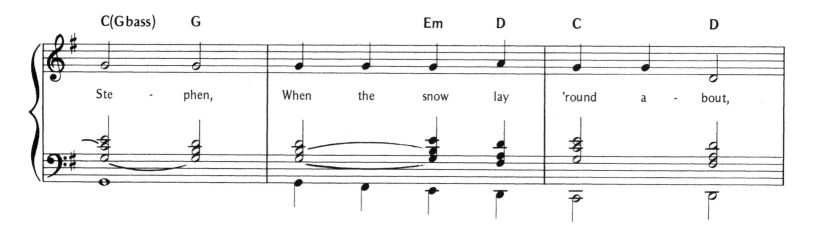

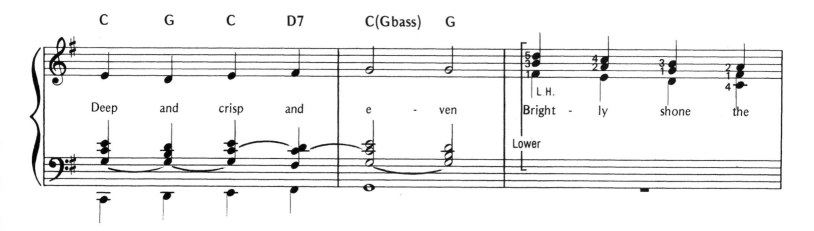

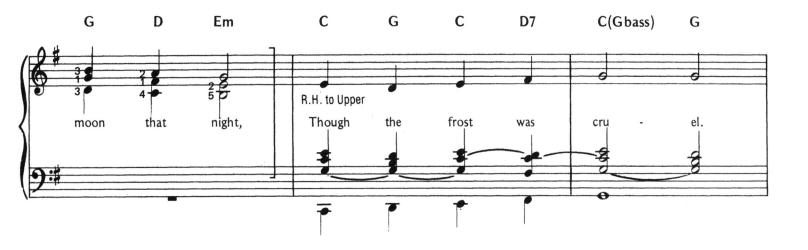

moon that night, Though the frost was cru - el.

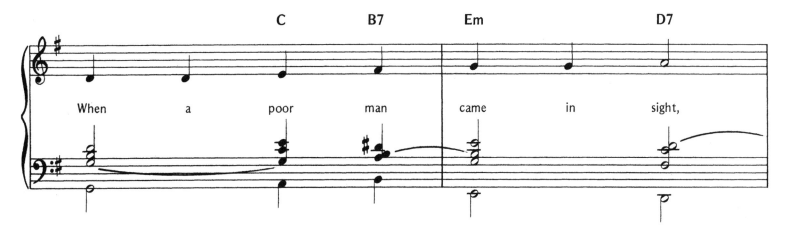

When a poor man came in sight,

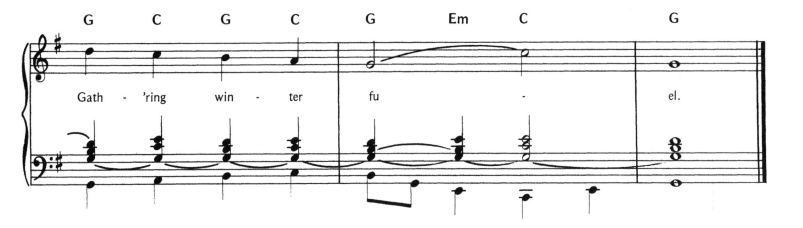

Gath - 'ring win - ter fu - el.

Hark! The Herald Angels Sing

Registration 8

Words by Charles Wesley
Altered by George Whitefield
Music by Felix Mendelssohn-Bartholdy
Arranged by William H. Cummings

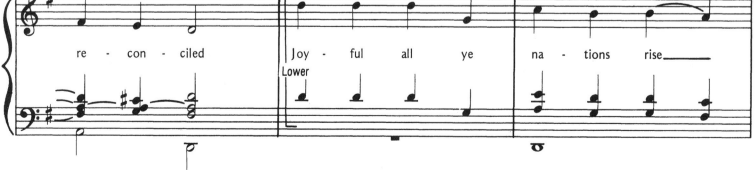

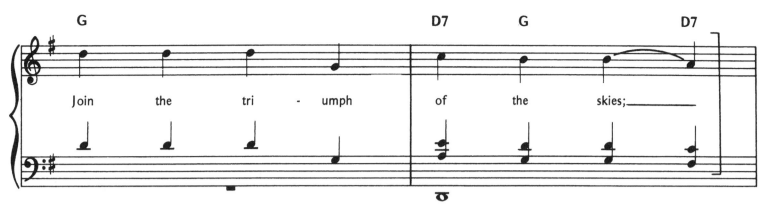

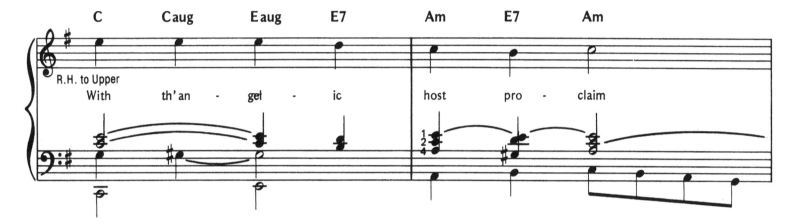

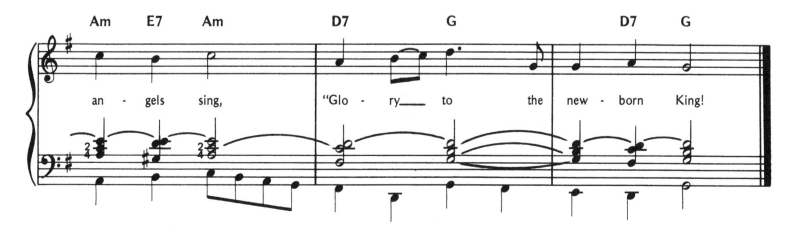

Have Yourself a Merry Little Christmas

from MEET ME IN ST. LOUIS

Registration 23

Words and Music by Hugh Martin
and Ralph Blane

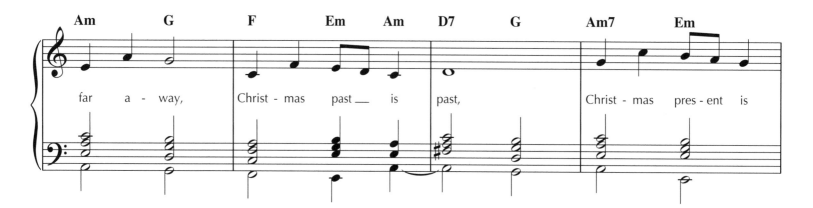

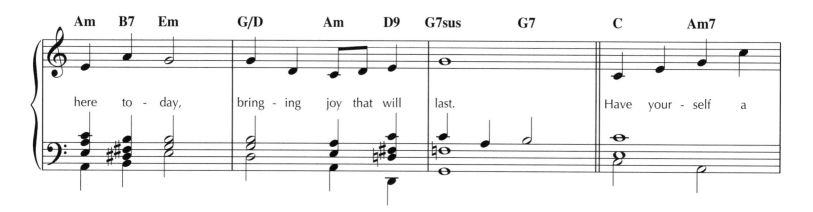

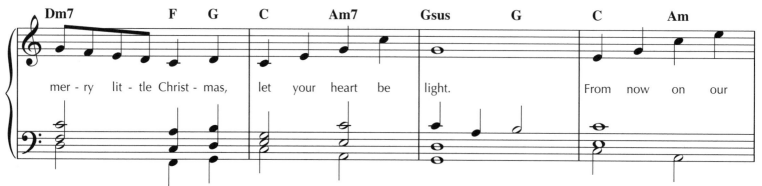

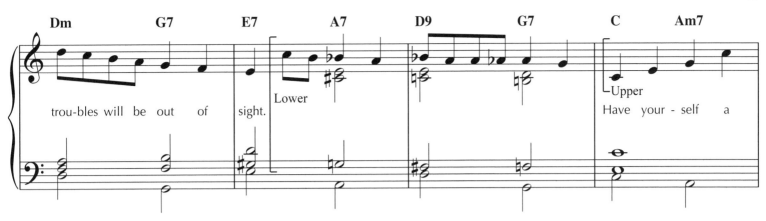

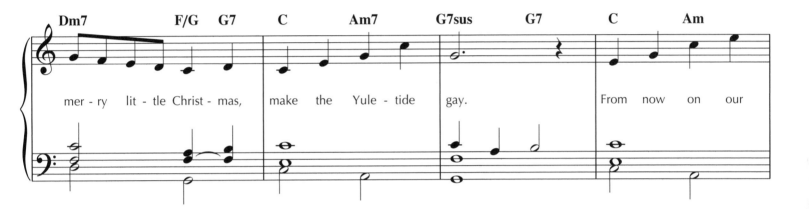

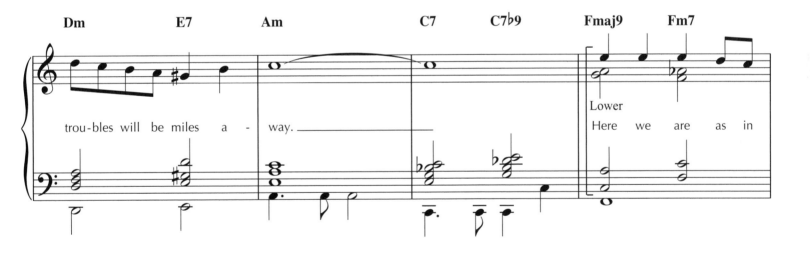

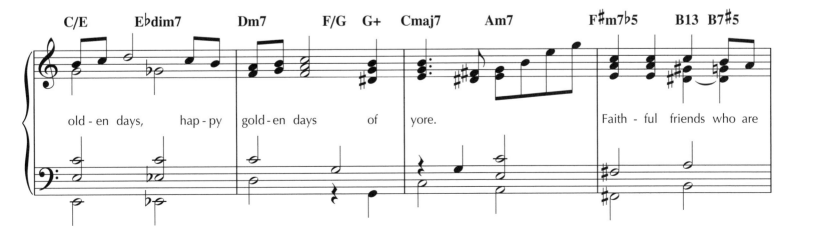

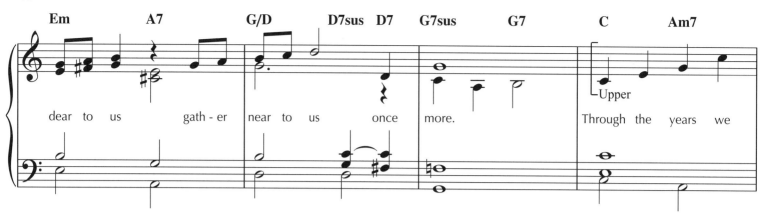

dear to us gath-er near to us once more. Through the years we

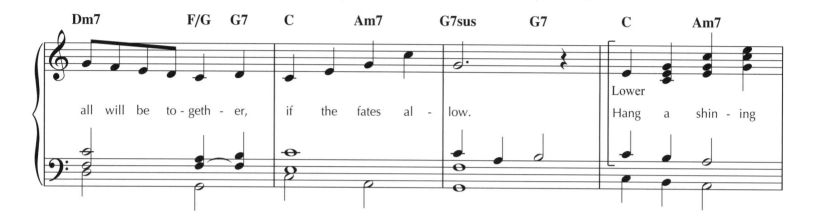

all will be to-geth-er, if the fates al-low. Hang a shin-ing

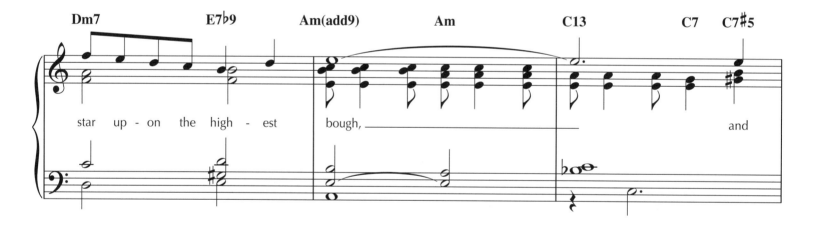

star up-on the high-est bough, and

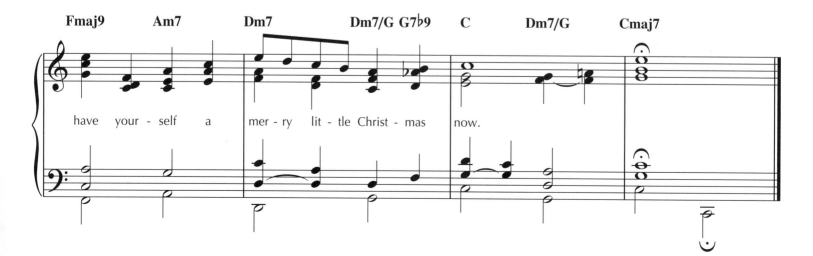

have your-self a mer-ry lit-tle Christ-mas now.

The Holly and the Ivy

Registration 13

18th Century English Carol

Here We Come A-Wassailing

Registration 2

Traditional English Carol

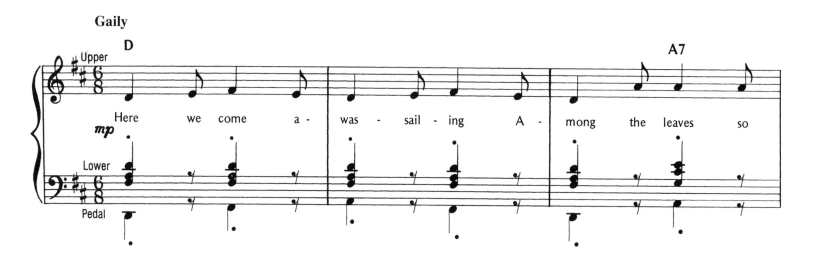

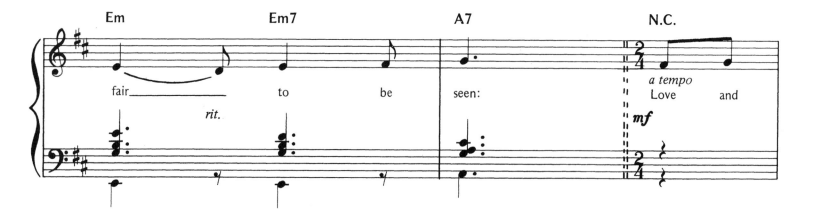

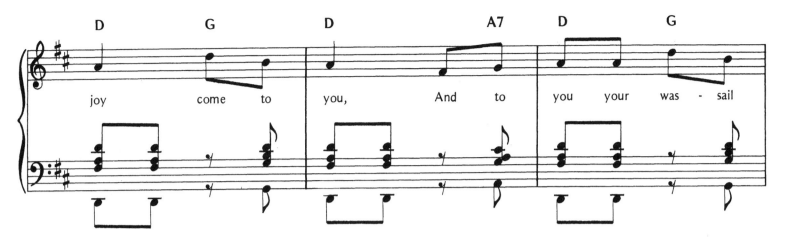

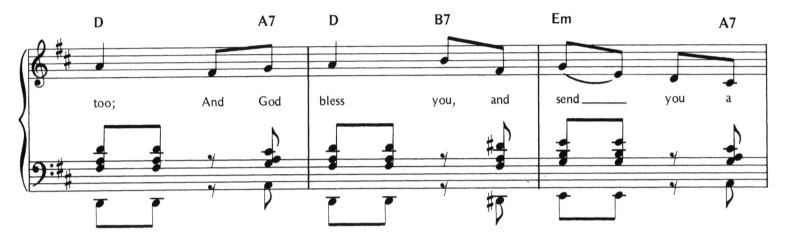

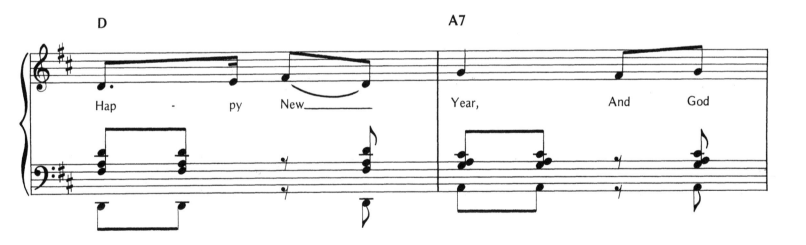

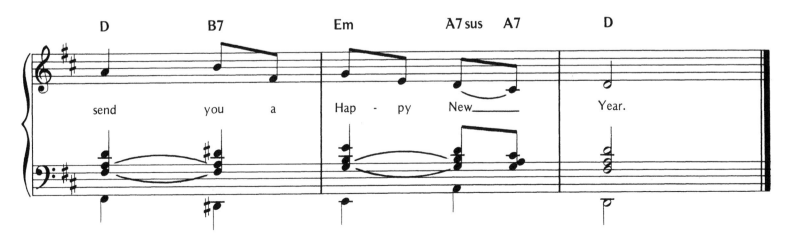

A Holly Jolly Christmas

Registration 46

Music and Lyrics by
Johnny Marks

Moderately bright

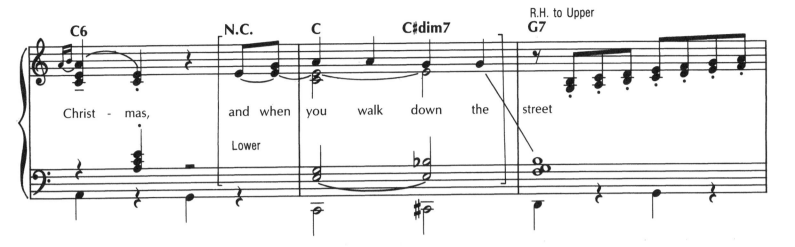

Christ - mas, and when you walk down the street

Lower

R.H. to Upper

Say hel - lo to friends you know and ev - 'ry - one you

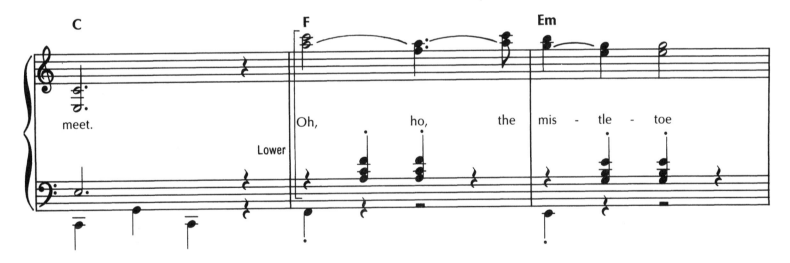

meet. Oh, ho, the mis - tle - toe

Lower

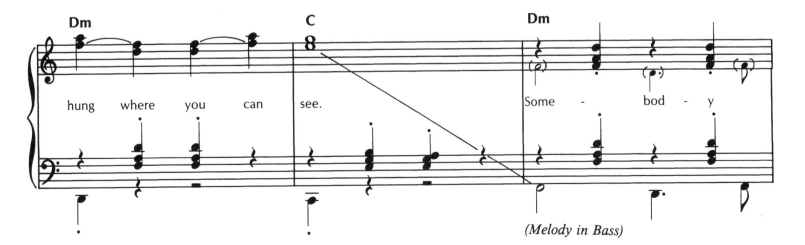

hung where you can see. Some - bod - y

(Melody in Bass)

(There's No Place Like)
Home for the Holidays

Registration 52

Words and Music by Al Stillman
and Robert Allen

Moderately, with feeling

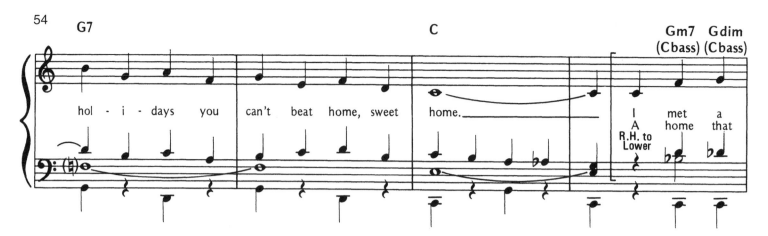

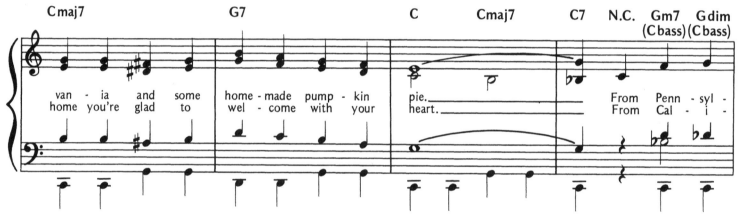

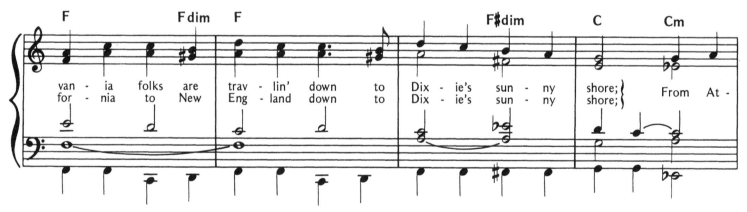

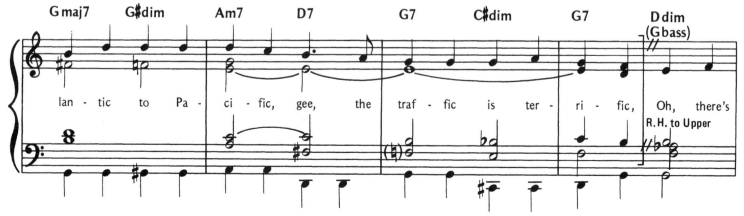

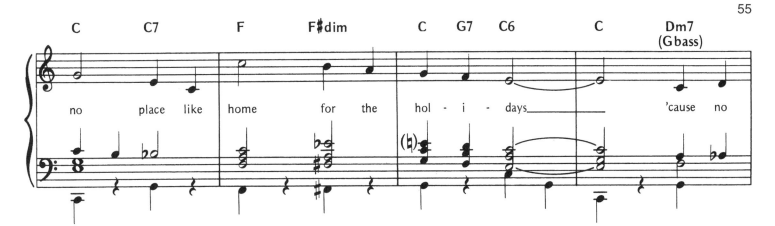

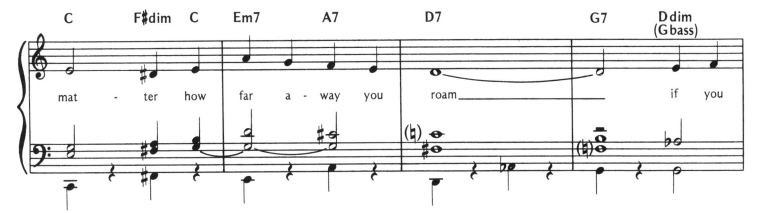

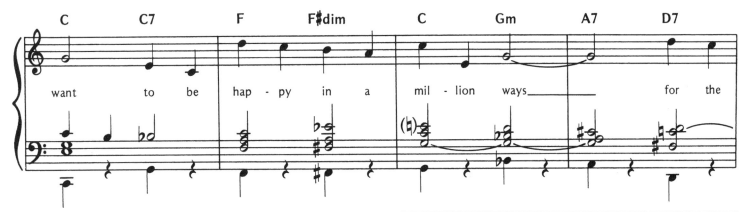

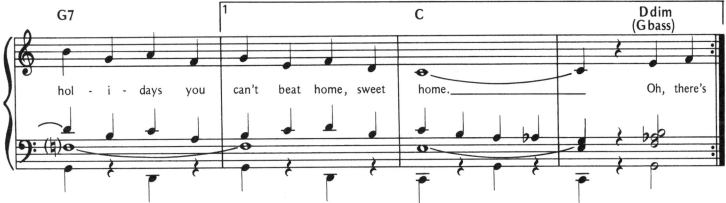

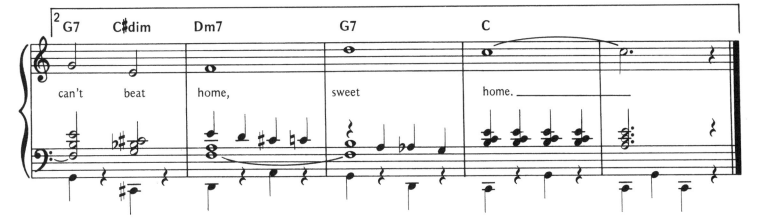

I Am So Glad on Christmas Eve

Registration 15

Words by Marie Wexelsen
Music by Peder Knudsen

I Heard the Bells on Christmas Day

Registration 37

Words by Henry Wadsworth Longfellow
Music by John Baptiste Calkin

Additional Lyrics

3. And in despair I bow'd my head:
   "There is no peace on earth," I said,
   "For hate is strong, and mocks the song
   Of peace on earth, good will to men."

4. Then pealed the bells more loud and deep:
   "God is not dead, nor doth He sleep;
   The wrong shall fail, the right prevail,
   With peace on earth, good will to men."

5. Till, ringing, singing on its way,
   The world revolved from night to day,
   A voice, a chime, a chant sublime,
   Of peace on earth, good will to men!

I Saw Mommy Kissing Santa Claus

Registration 26

Words and Music by
Tommie Connor

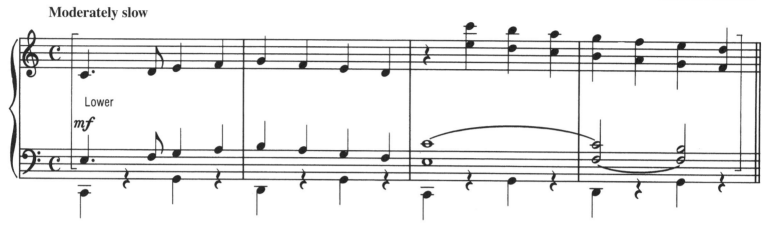

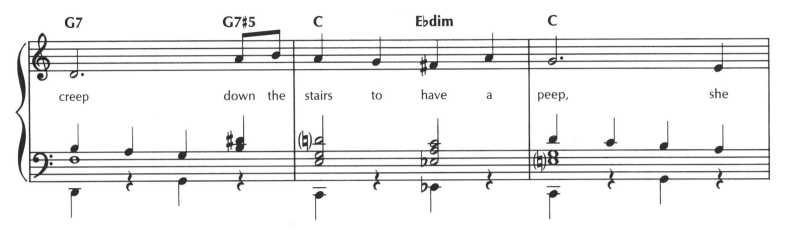

creep down the stairs to have a peep, she

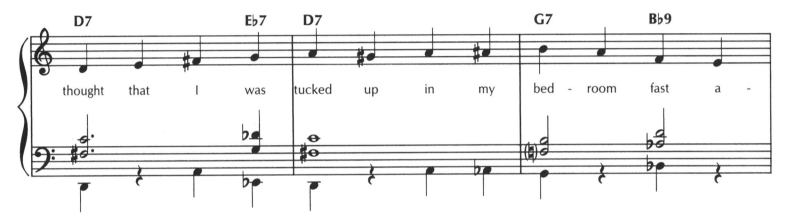

thought that I was tucked up in my bed - room fast a -

sleep. Then I saw Mom - my tick - le

R.H. to Upper

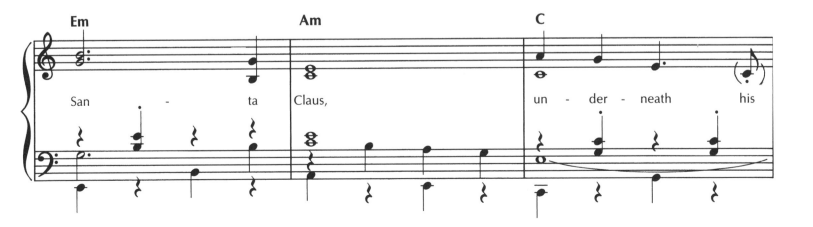

San - ta Claus, un - der - neath his

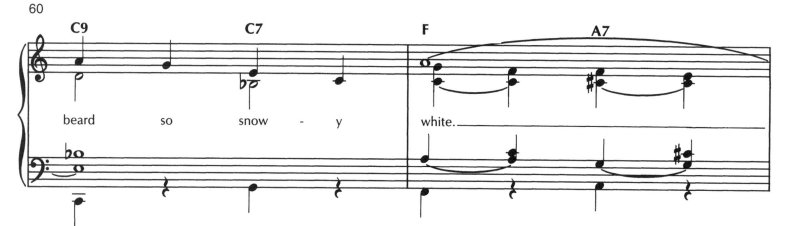

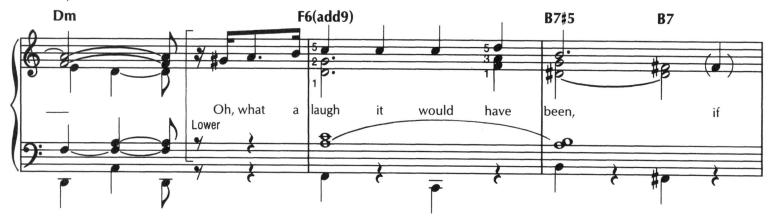

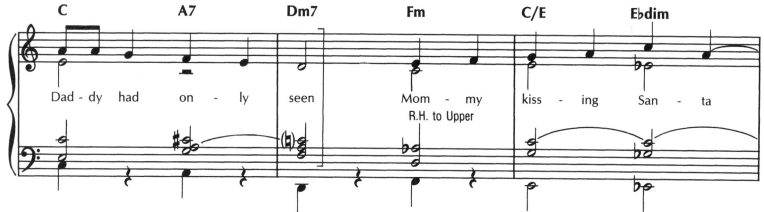

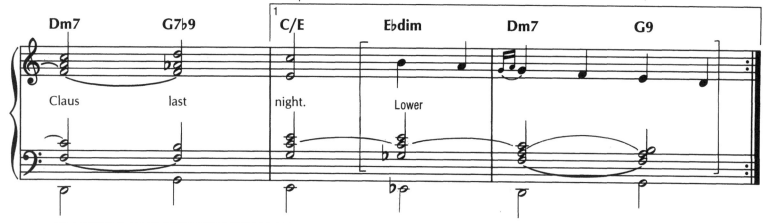

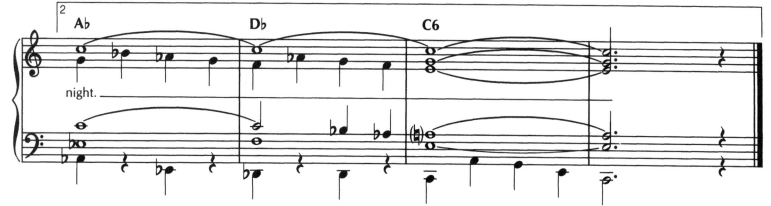

I Saw Three Ships

Registration 1

Traditional English Carol

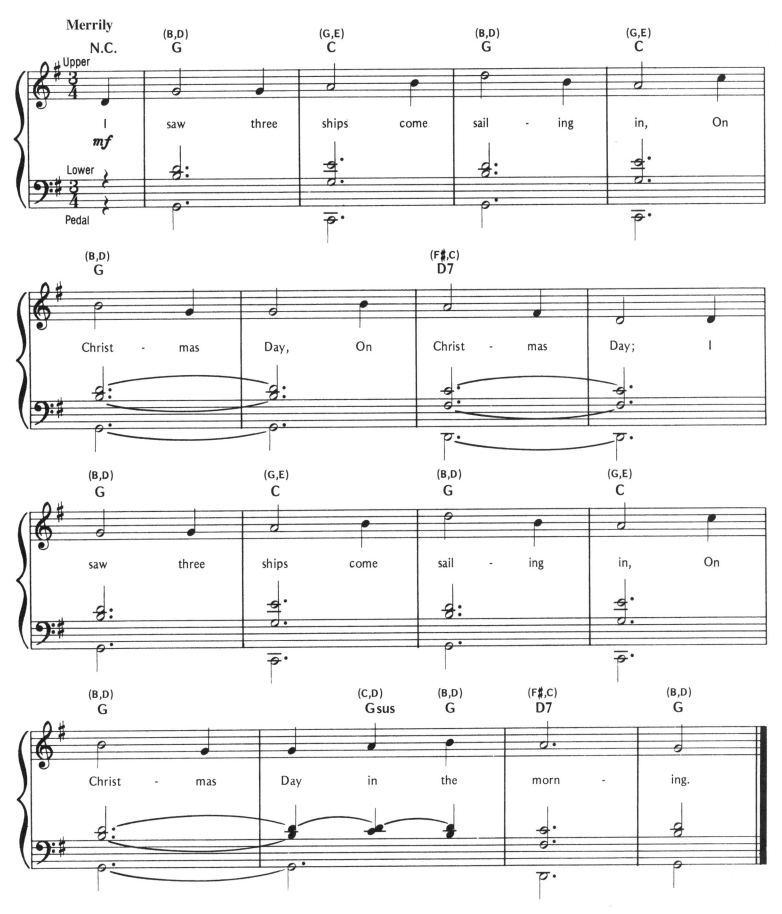

I'll Be Home for Christmas

Registration 44

Words and Music by Kim Gannon
and Walter Kent

Moderately slow (ad lib.)

I'm dream-ing to-night of a place I love,___ Ev-en more than I u-sual-ly do. And al-though I know it's a long road back,___ I prom-ise you

With a steady beat

I'll be Home For Christ-mas___

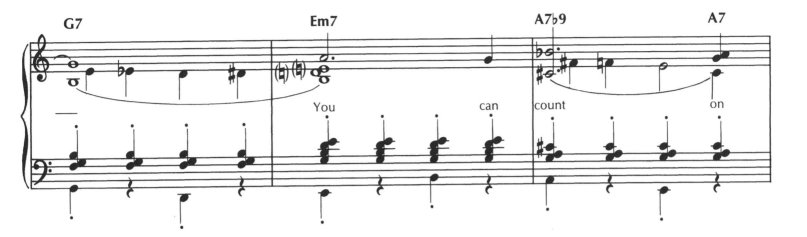

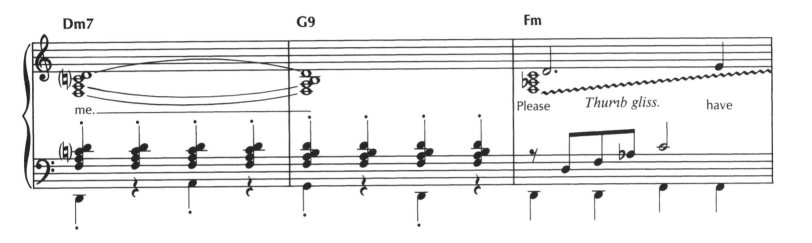

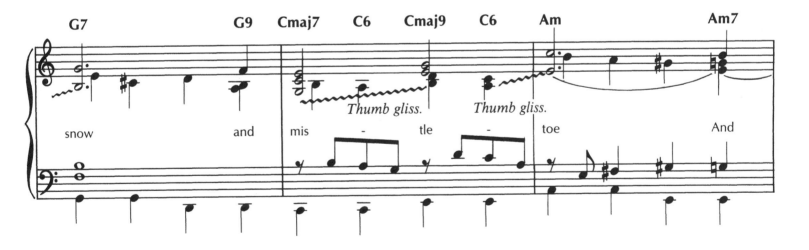

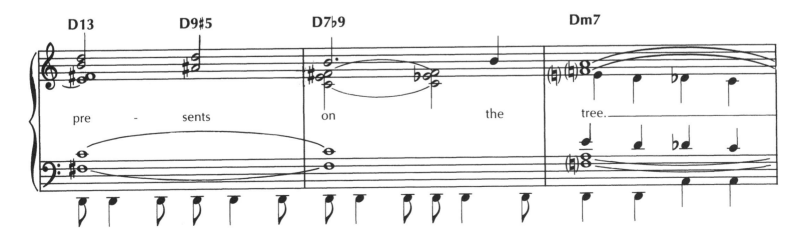

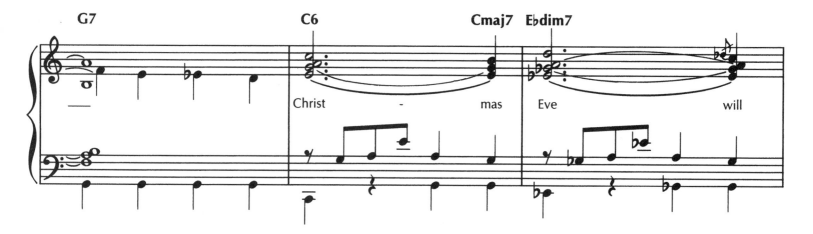

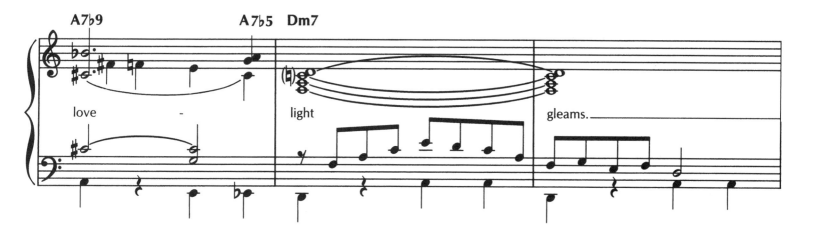

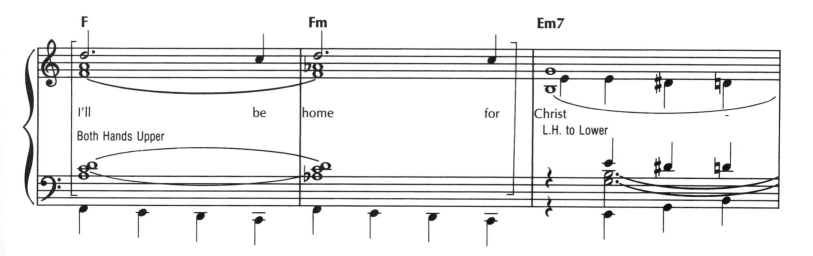

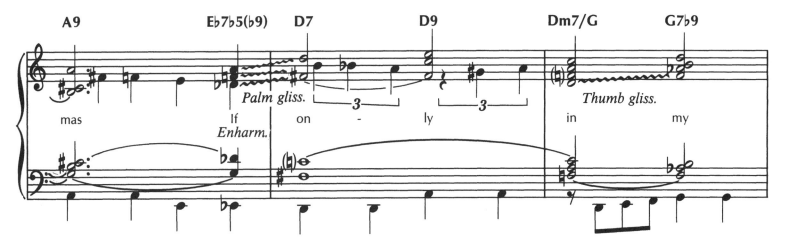

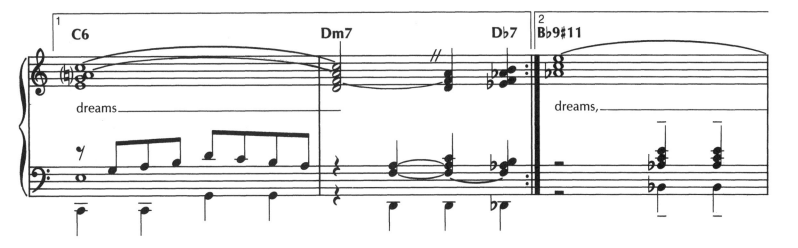

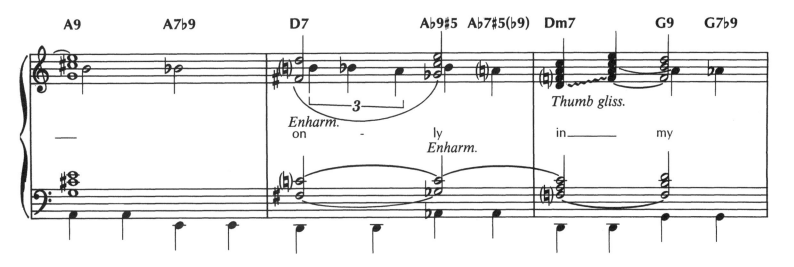

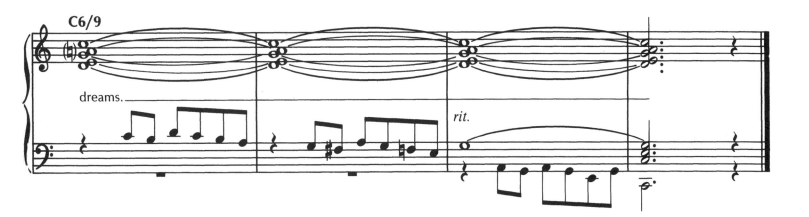

In a Manger He Is Lying

Registration6

Traditional Polish Carol

In the Bleak Midwinter

Registration 17

Poem by Christina Rossetti
Music by Gustav Holst

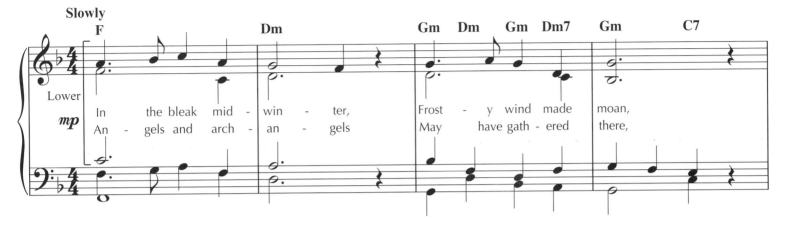

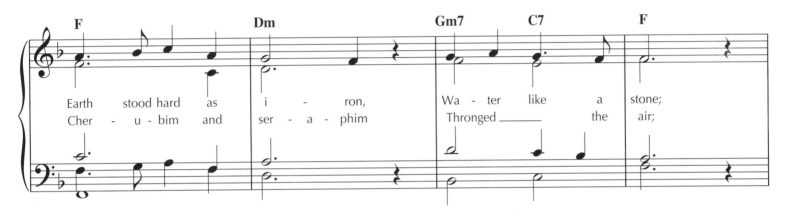

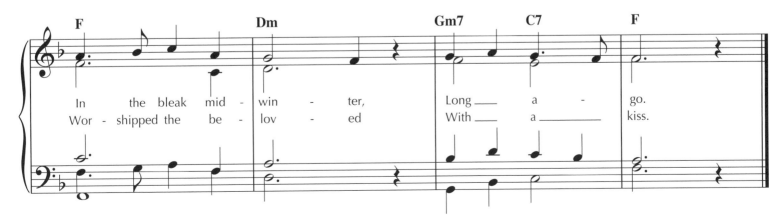

It Came Upon the Midnight Clear

Registration 4

Words by Edmund Hamilton Sears
Music by Richard Storrs Willis

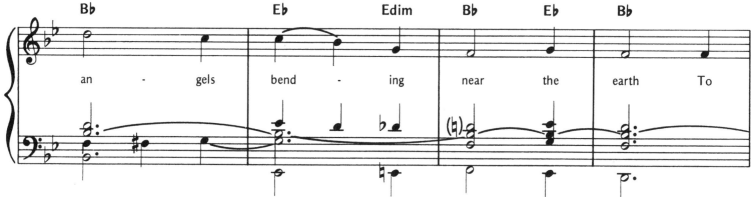

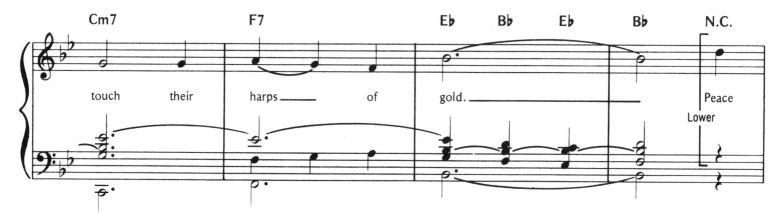

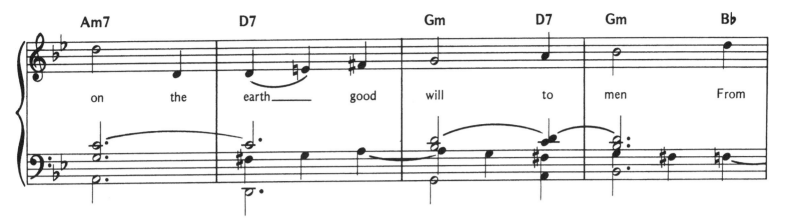

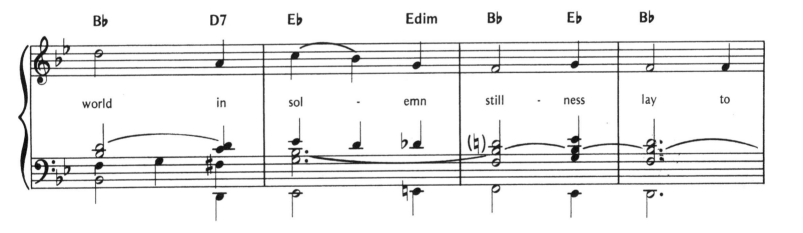

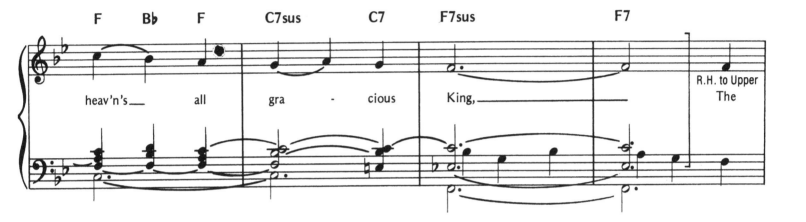

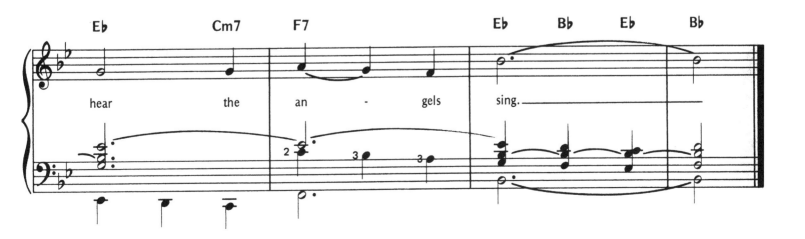

Jingle Bell Rock

Registration 49

Words and Music by Joe Beal
and Jim Boothe

Moderately, with a beat

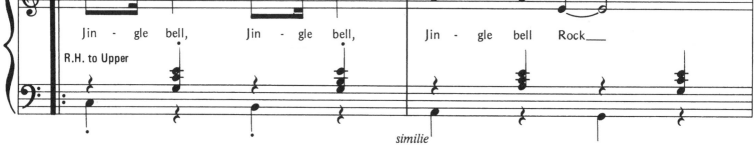

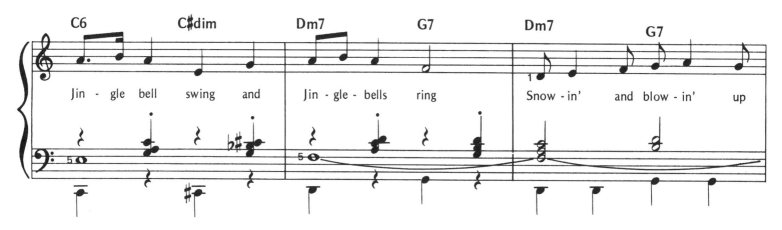

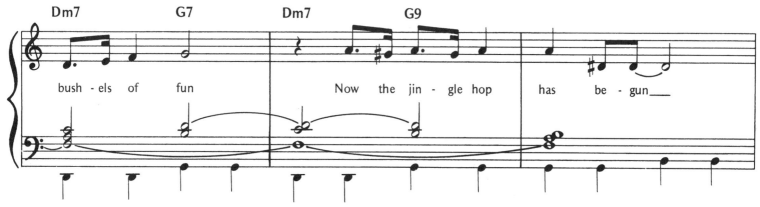

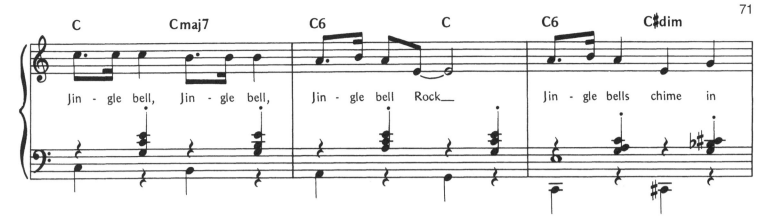

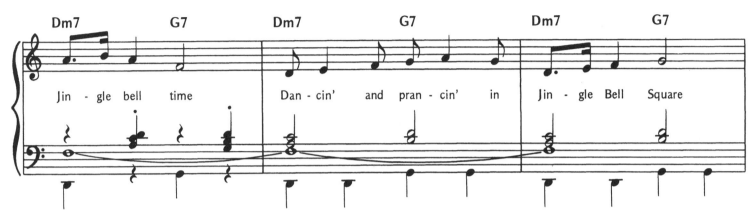

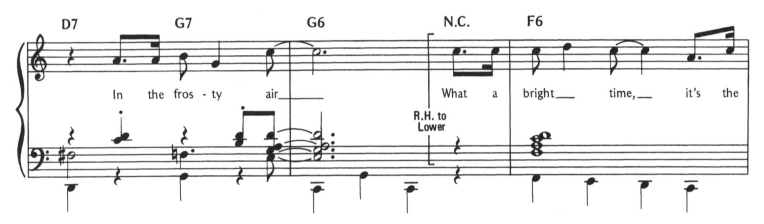

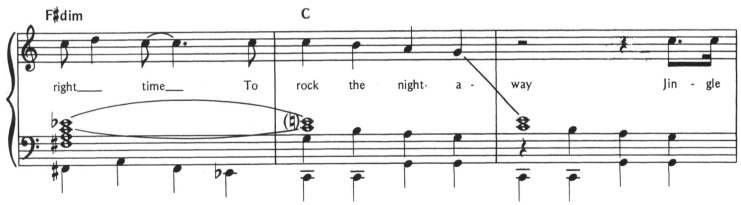

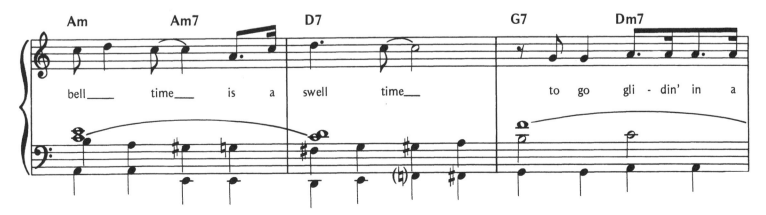

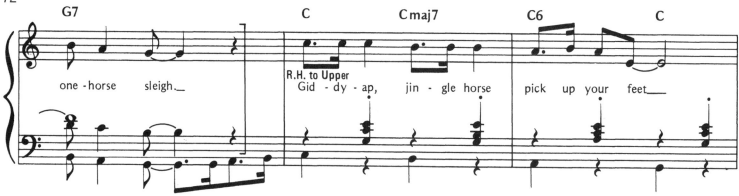

one-horse sleigh.___ Gid-dy-ap, jin-gle horse pick up your feet___

R.H. to Upper

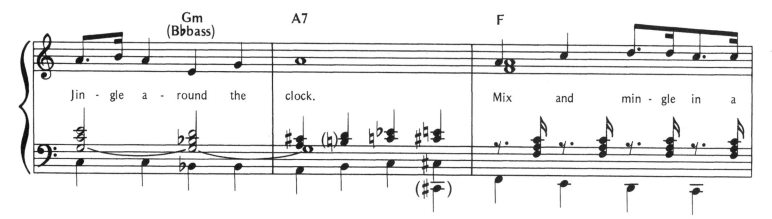

Jin - gle a - round the clock. Mix and min - gle in a

jin - gle - in' beat___ That's the Jin - gle bell Rock.___

That's the Jin - gle bell That's the Jin - gle bell

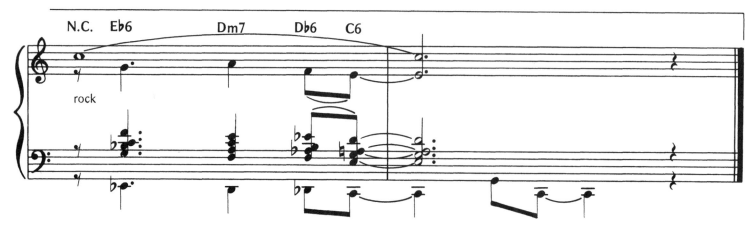

rock

Jolly Old St. Nicholas

Registration 15

Traditional 19th Century American Carol

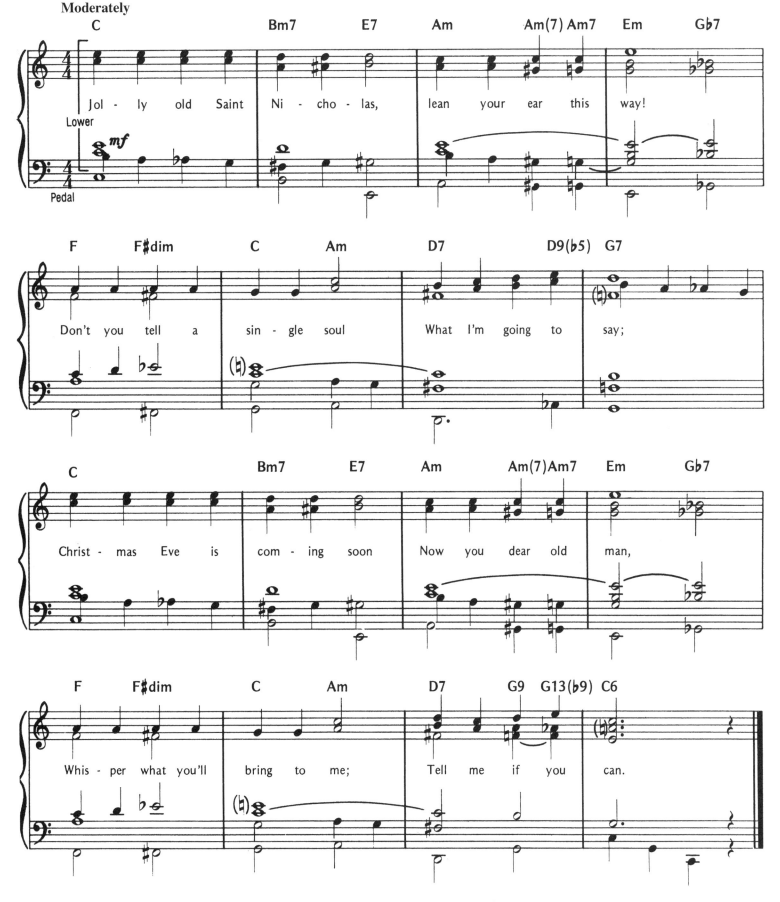

Jingle Bells

Registration 19

Words and Music by
J. Pierpont

Moderately fast

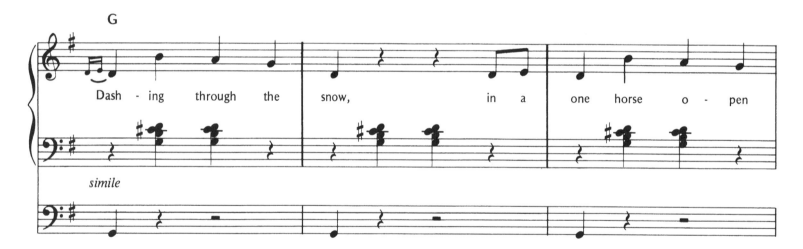

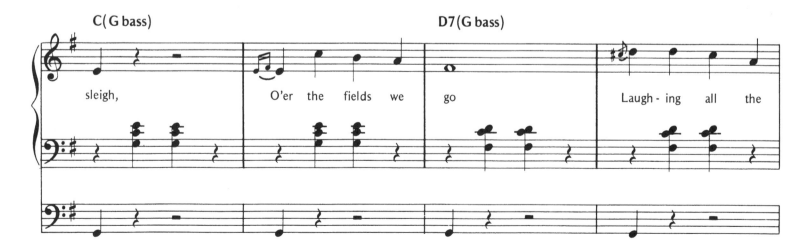

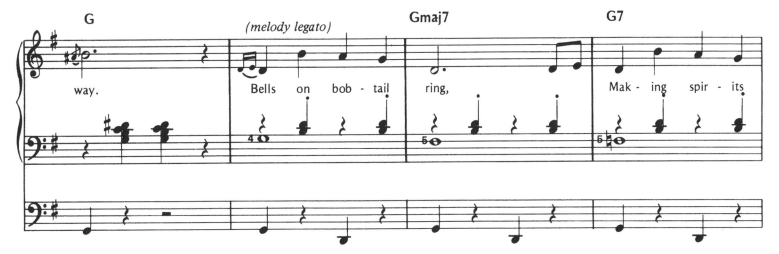

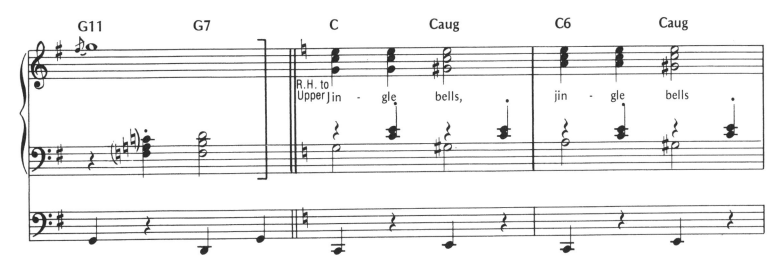

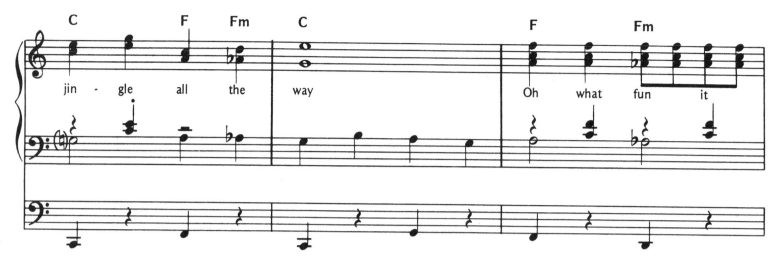

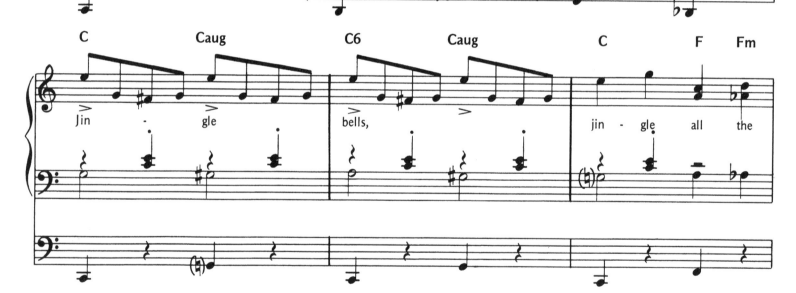

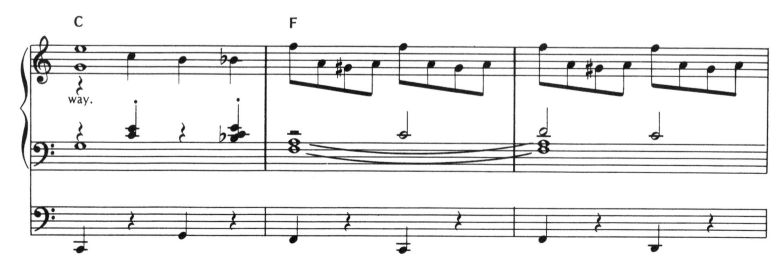

Joy to the World

Registraton 7

Words by Isaac Watts
Music by George Frideric Handel
Adapted by Lowell Mason

With spirit

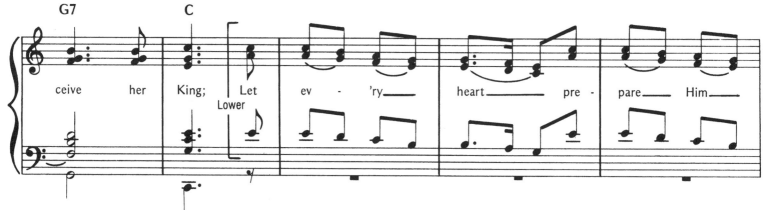

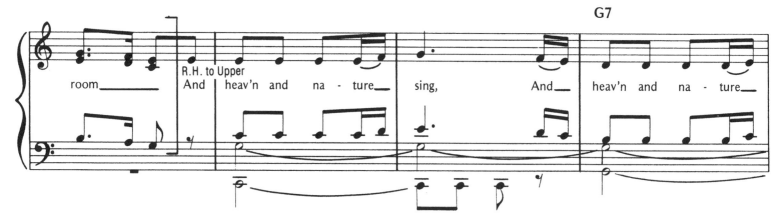

Let It Snow! Let It Snow! Let It Snow!

Registration 38

Words by Sammy Cahn
Music by Jule Styne

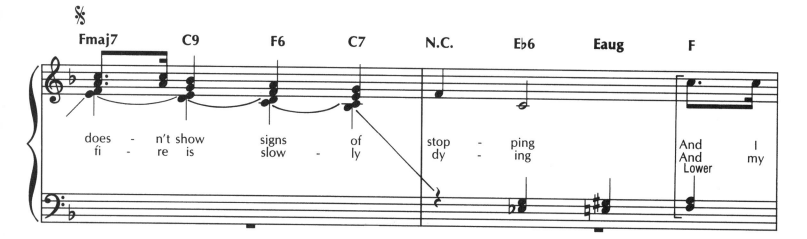

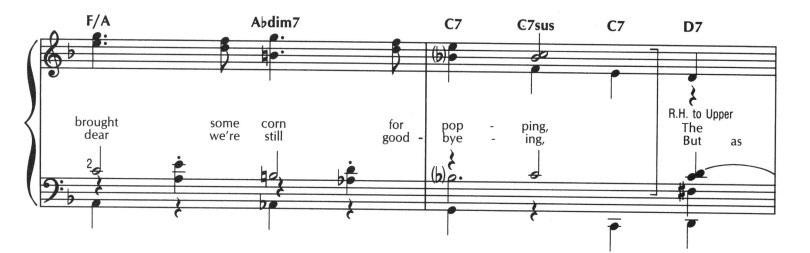

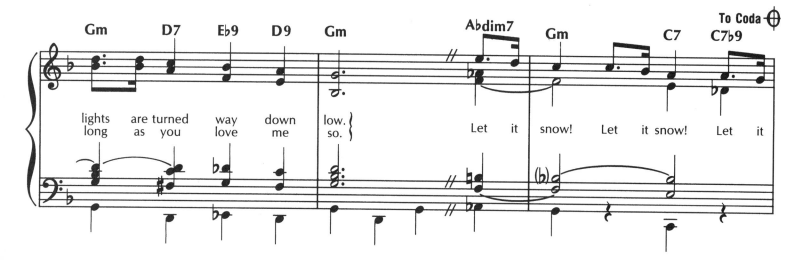

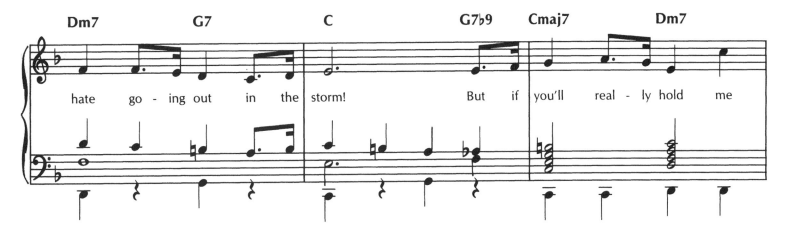

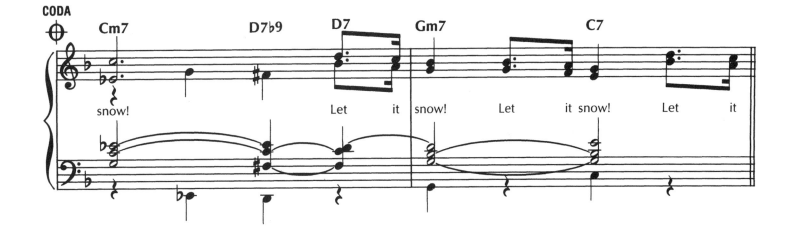

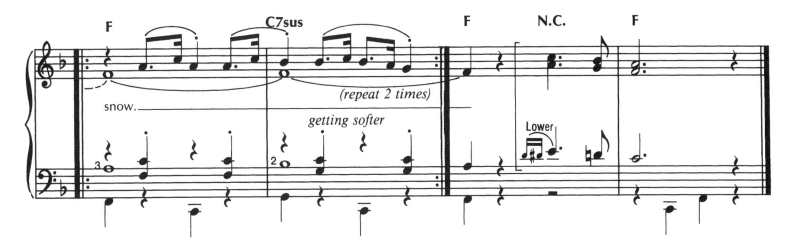

March of the Toys
from BABES IN TOYLAND

Registration 7

By Victor Herbert

Moderately

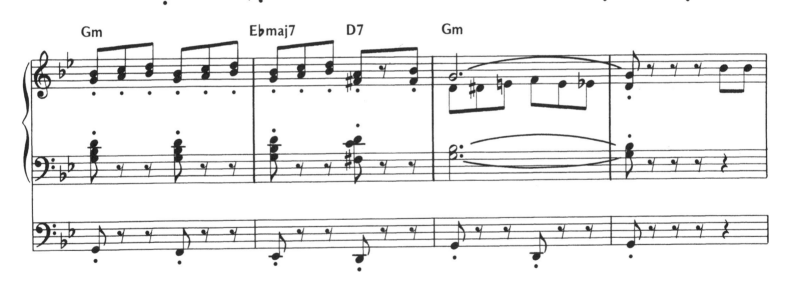

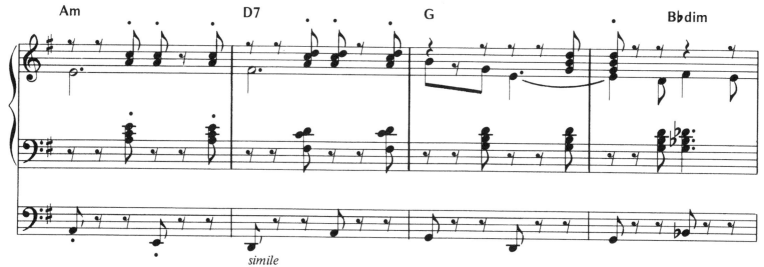

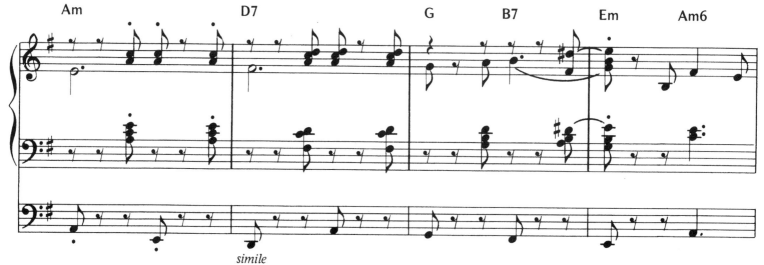

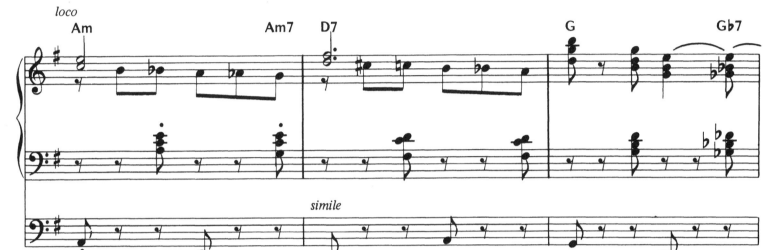

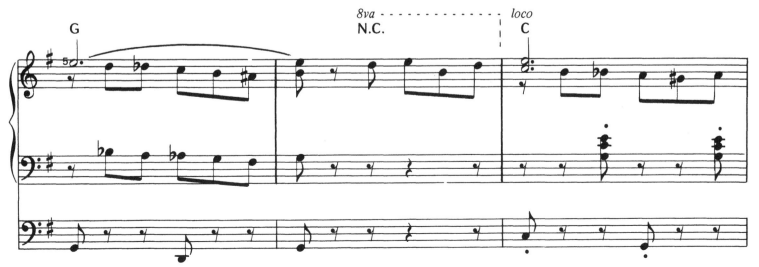

A Marshmallow World

Registration 29

Words by Carl Sigman
Music by Peter De Rose

*Enharmonic

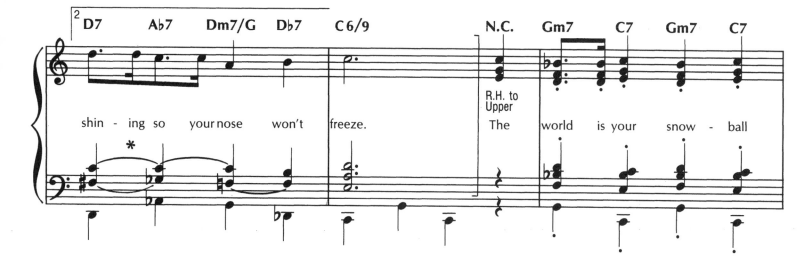

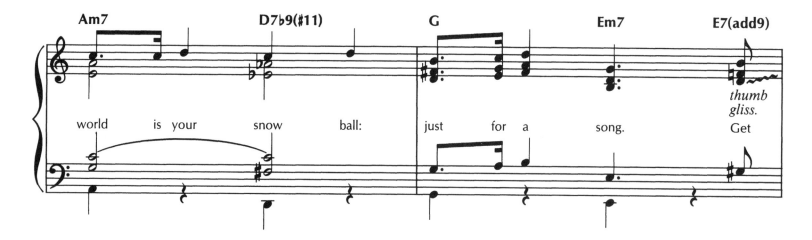

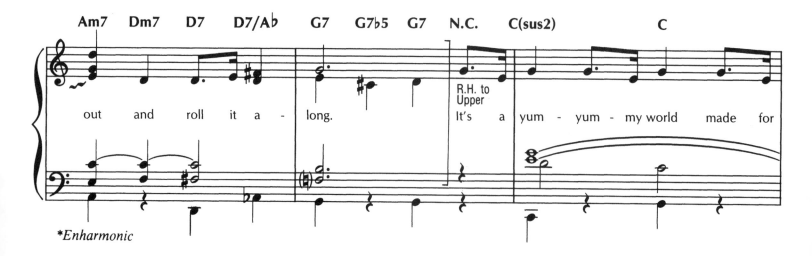

*Enharmonic

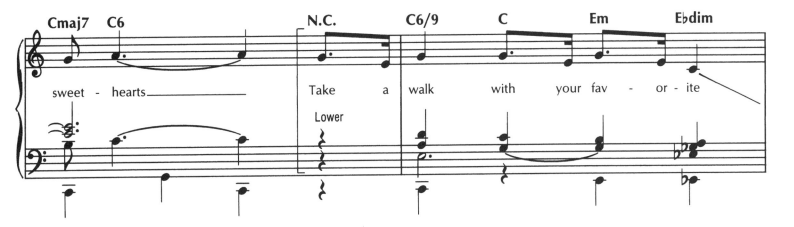

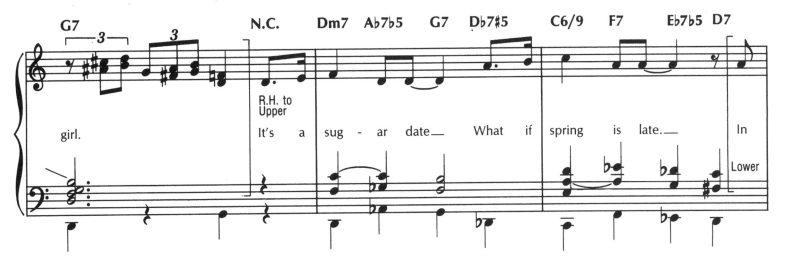

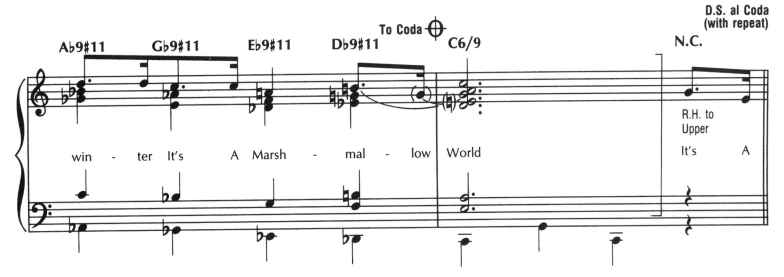

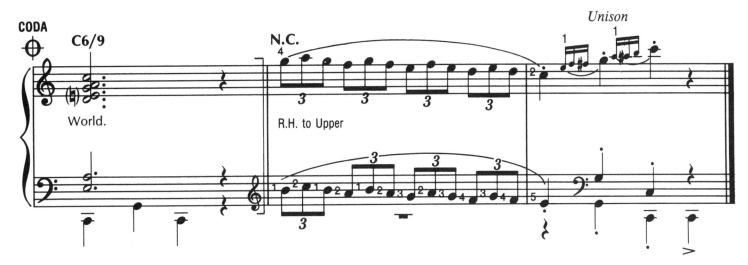

Mary Had a Baby

Registration 15

African-American Spiritual

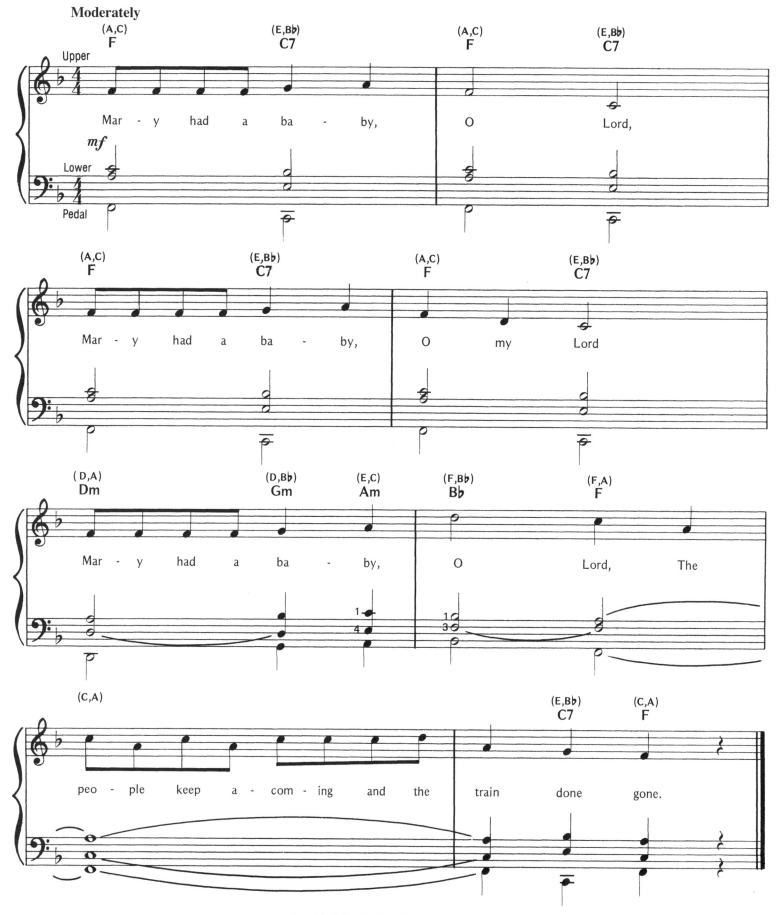

O Come, Little Children

Registration 3

Words by C. von Schmidt
Music by J.P.A. Schulz

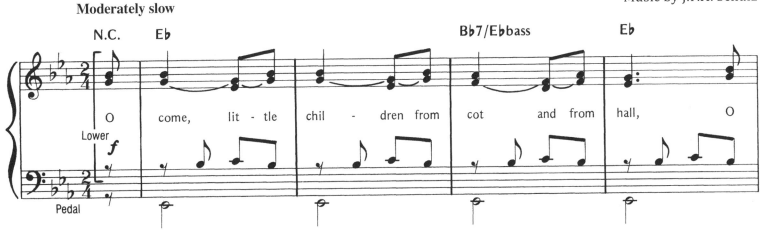

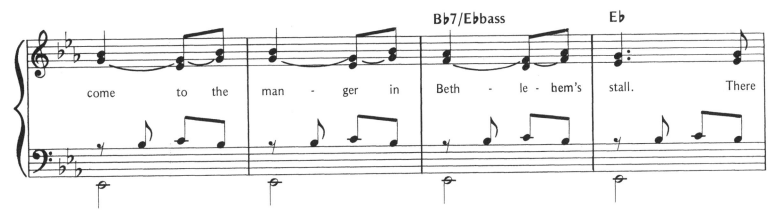

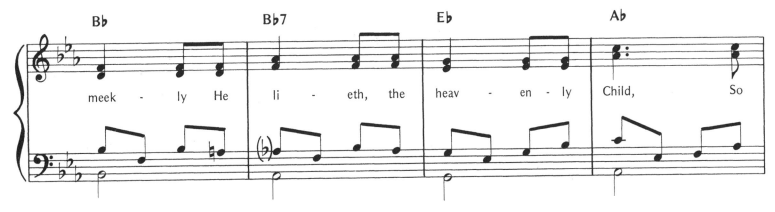

Masters in This Hall

Registration 7

Traditional English

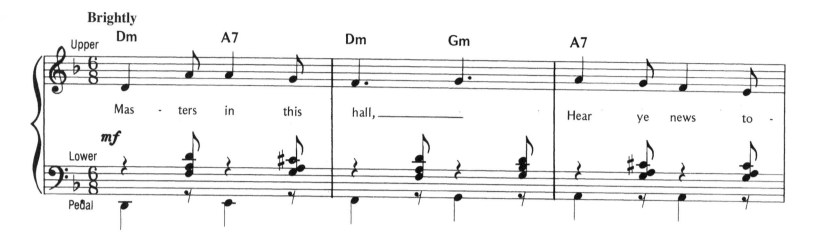

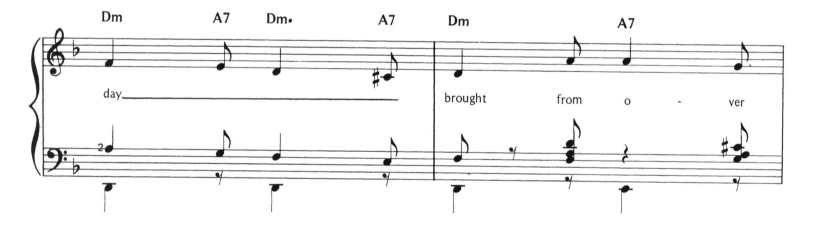

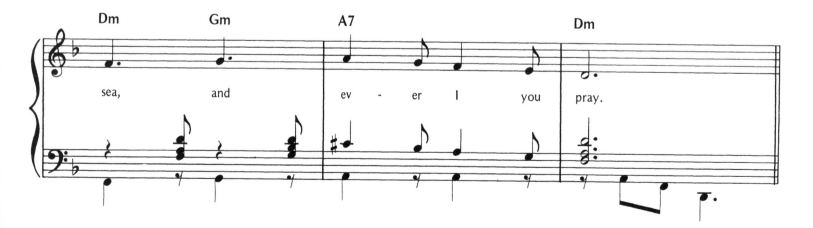

{ 1st time both hands lower manual }
{ 2nd time R.H. upper, L.H. lower }

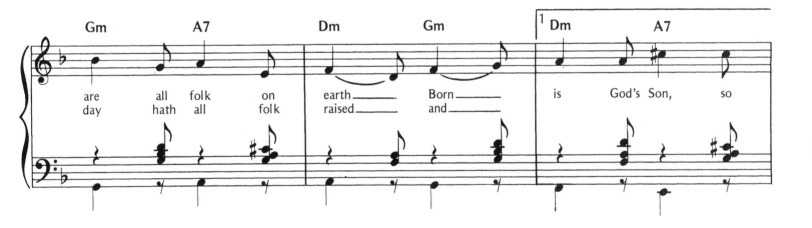

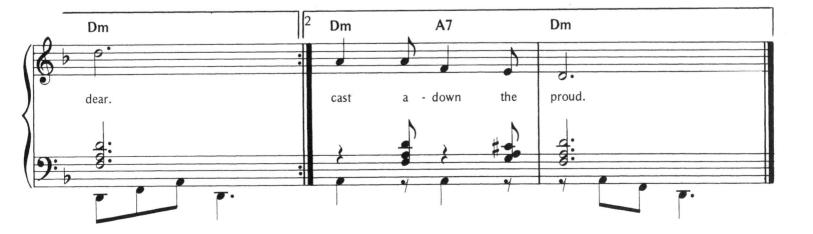

O Christmas Tree

Registration 13

Traditional German Carol

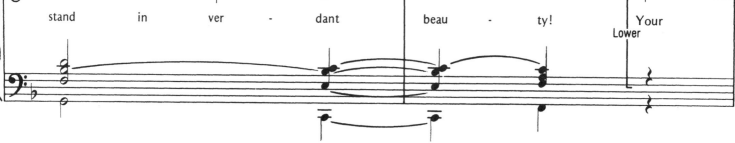

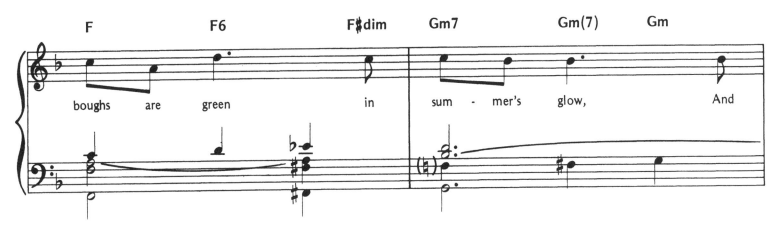

boughs are green in sum-mer's glow, And

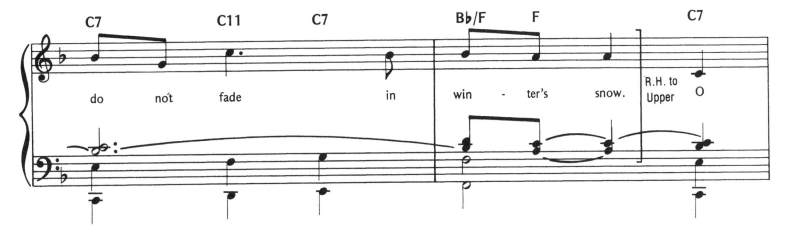

do not fade in win-ter's snow. R.H. to Upper O

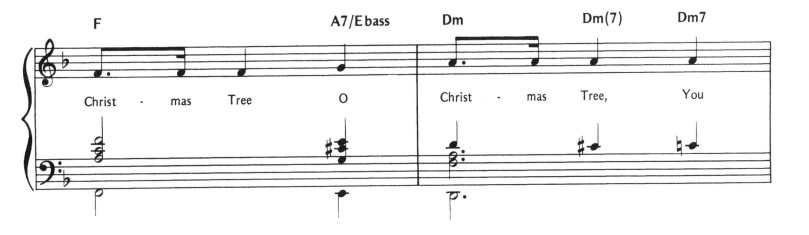

Christ - mas Tree O Christ - mas Tree, You

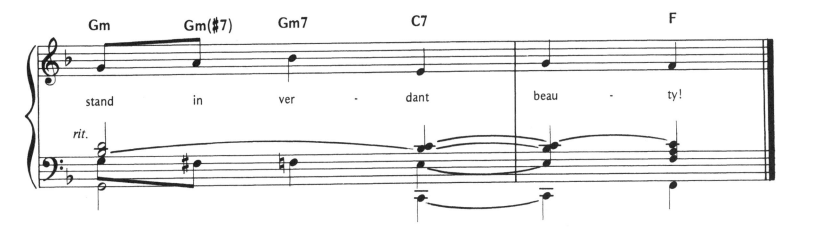

stand in ver - dant beau - ty!

O Come, All Ye Faithful
(Adeste fideles)

Registration 8

Music by John Francis Wade
Latin Words translated by Frederick Oakeley

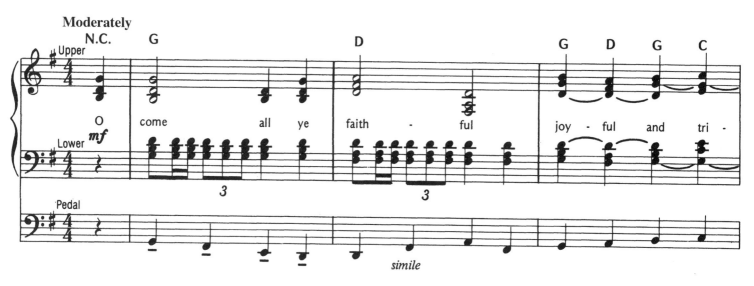

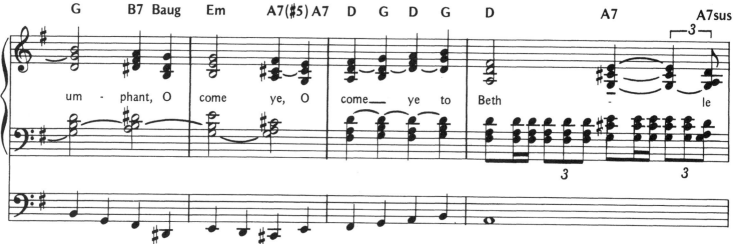

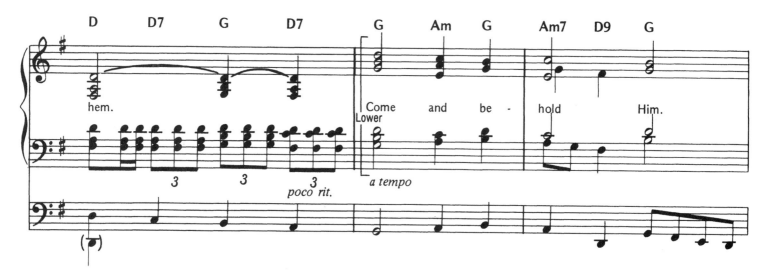

O Come, O Come, Immanuel

Registration 1

Plainsong, 13th Century
Words translated by John M. Neale
and Henry S. Coffin

O Holy Night

Registration 7

French Words by Placide Cappeau
English Words by John S. Dwight
Music by Adolphe Adam

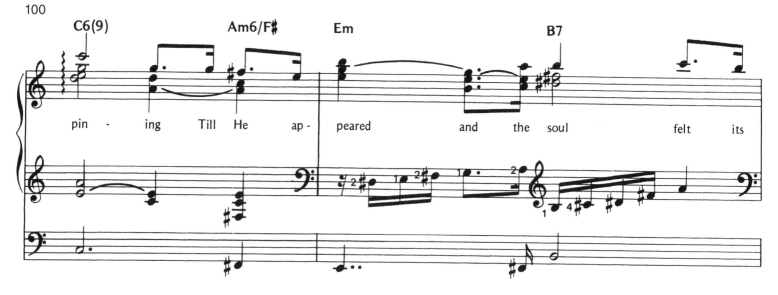

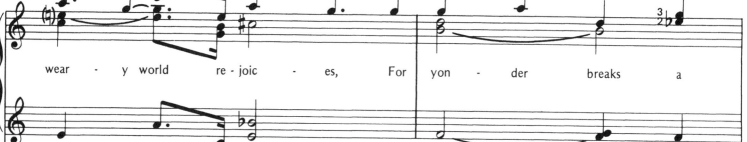

O Jesus So Sweet

Registration 1

Text by Valentin Thilo
Translated by Frieda Pietsch
German Hymn Tune

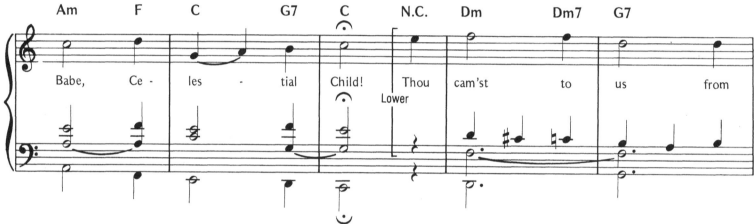

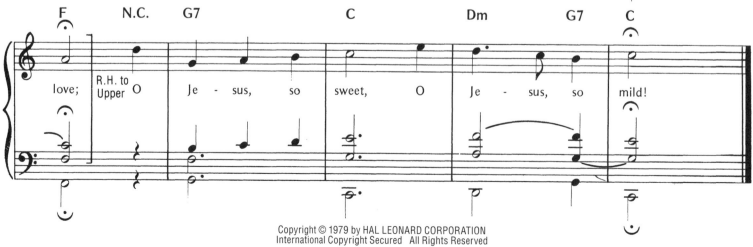

O Sanctissima

Registration 10

Sicilian Carol

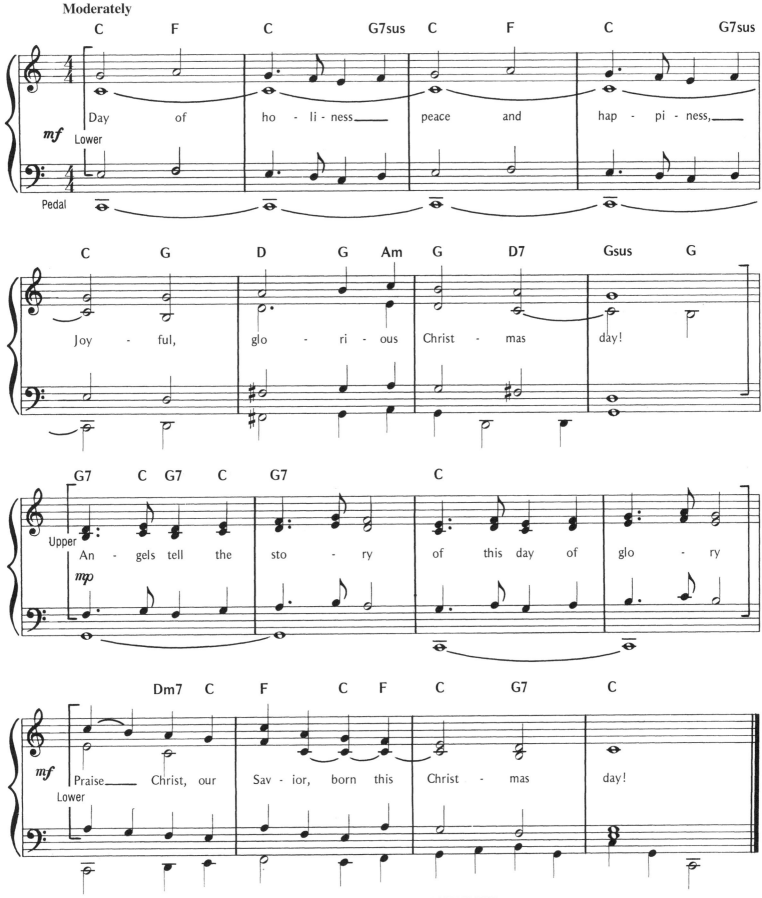

O Little Town of Bethlehem

Registration 4

Words by Phillips Brooks
Music by Lewis H. Redner

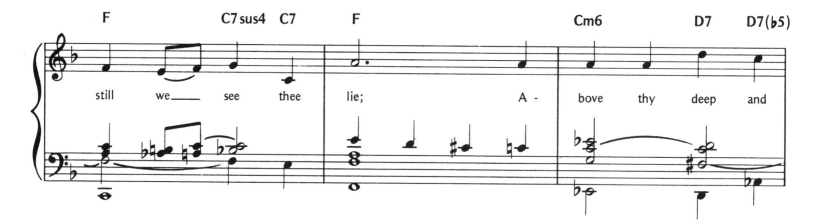

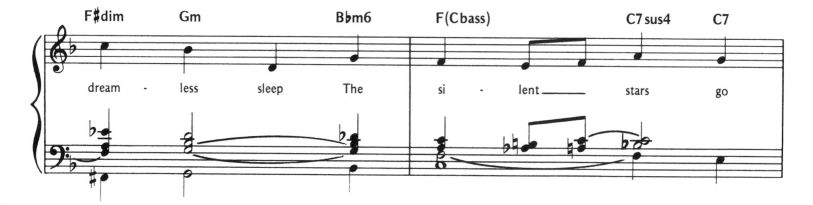

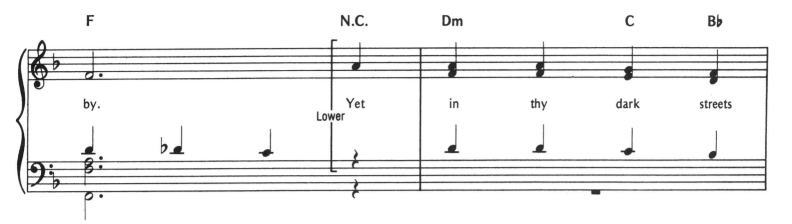

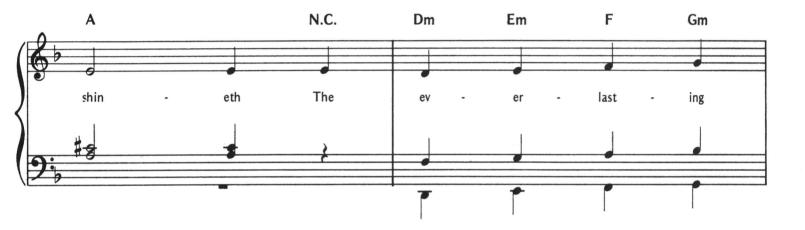

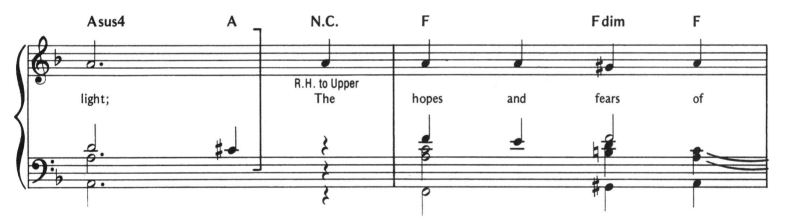

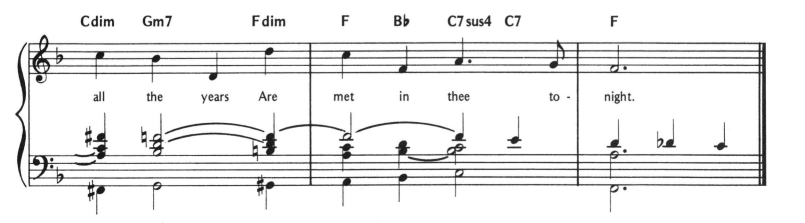

On Christmas Night

Registration 7

Sussex Carol

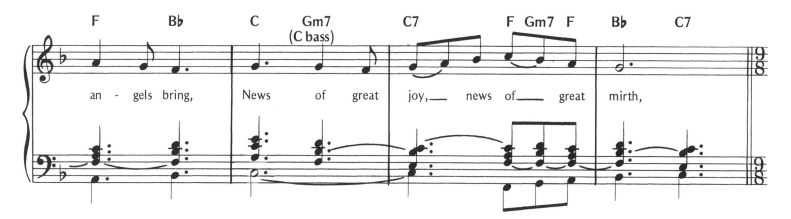

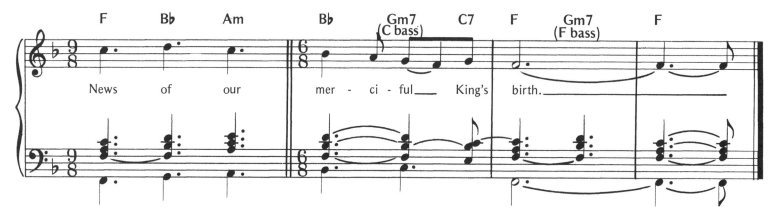

Once in Royal David's City

Registration 5

Words by Cecil F. Alexander
Music by Henry J. Gauntlett

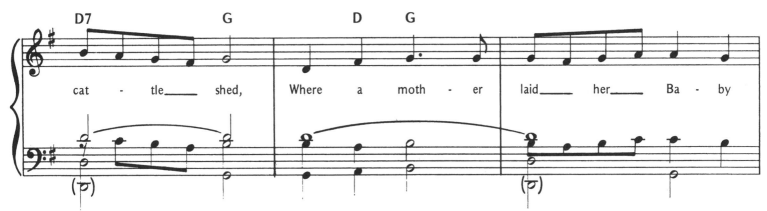

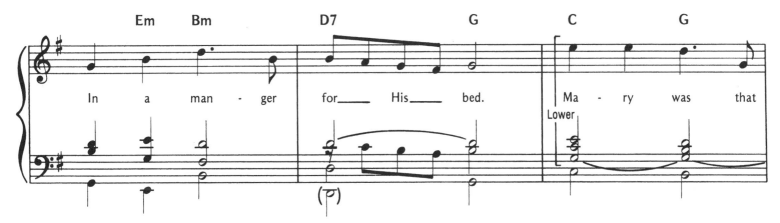

Pat-A-Pan
(Willie, Take Your Little Drum)

Registration 17

Words and Music by
Bernard de la Monnoye

Rockin' Around the Christmas Tree

Registration 46

Music and Lyrics by
Johnny Marks

110

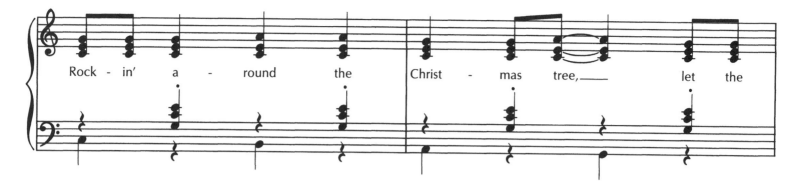

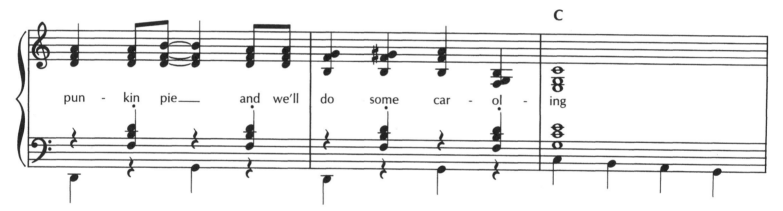

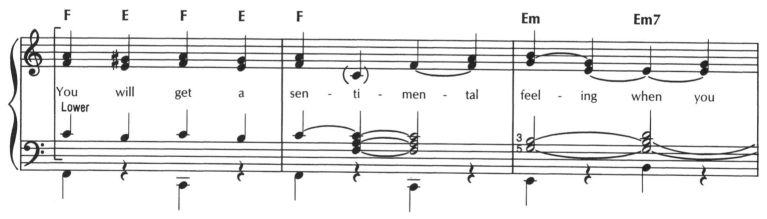

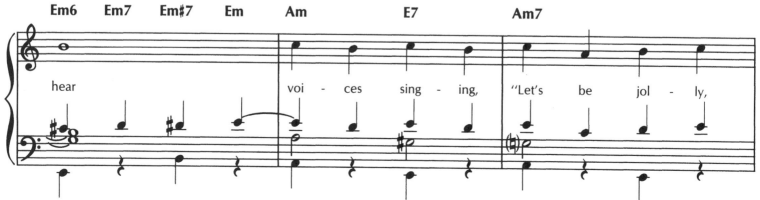

111

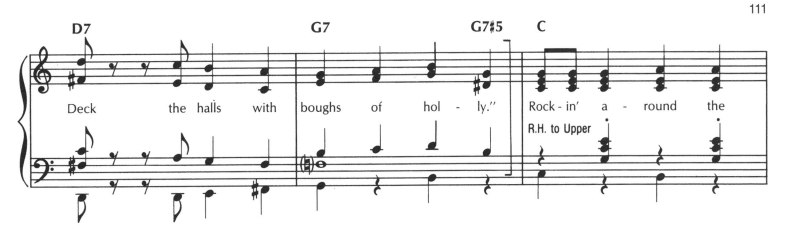

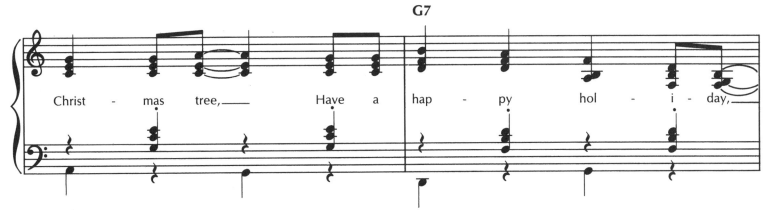

Rise Up, Shepherd, and Follow

Registration 13

African-American Spiritual

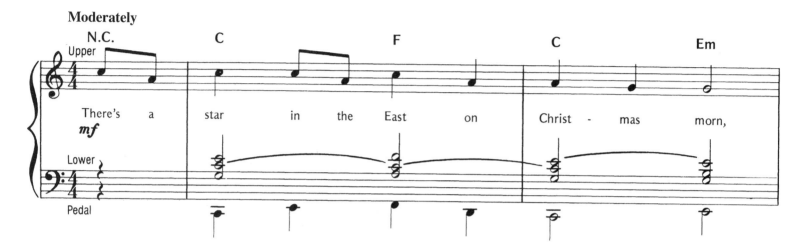

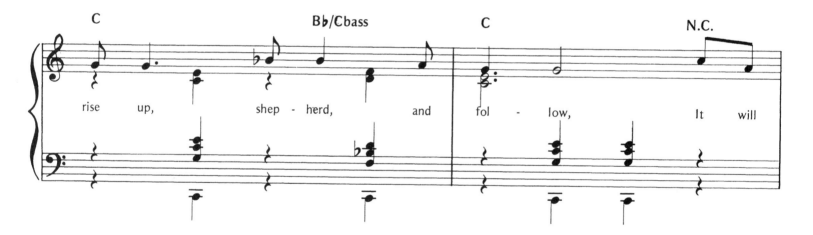

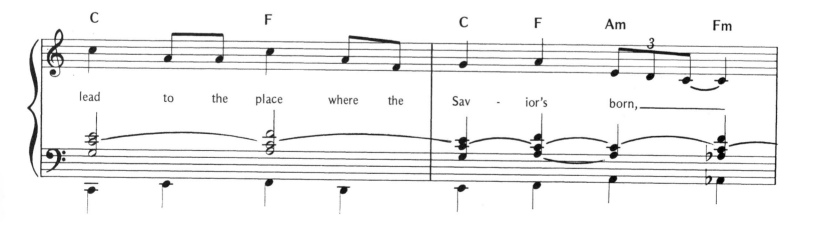

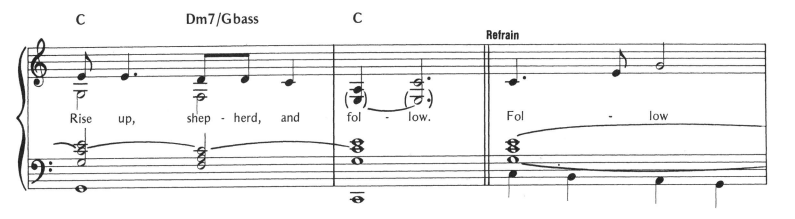

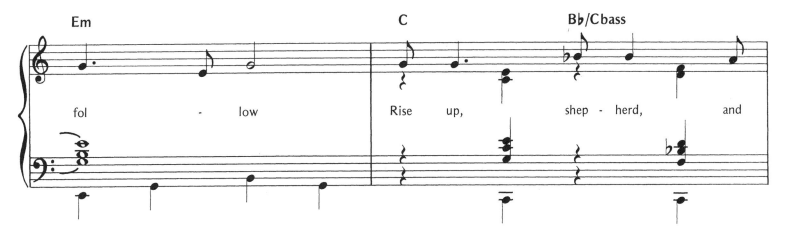

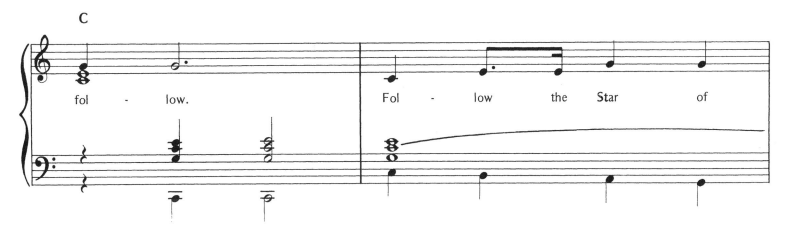

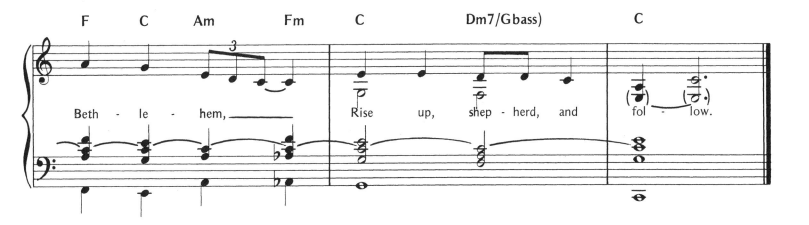

Rudolph the Red-Nosed Reindeer

Registration 33

Music and Lyrics by
Johnny Marks

Lightly

You know Dash - er and Danc - er and Pranc - er and Vix - en,

Com - et and Cu - pid and Don - ner and Blitz - en but do you re-

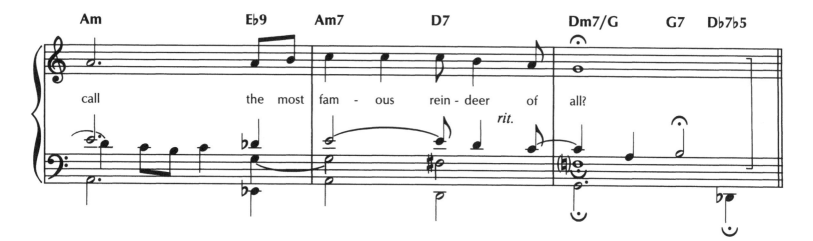

call the most fam - ous rein - deer of all?

With a steady beat

CHORUS

Ru - dolph, the red - nosed rein - deer

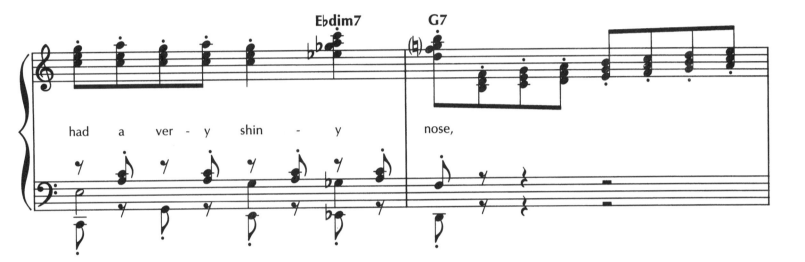

had a ver - y shin - y nose,

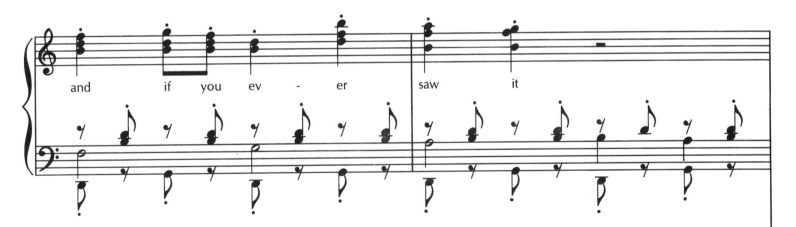

and if you ev - er saw it

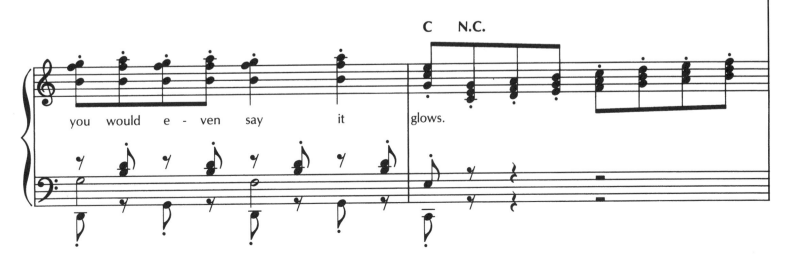

you would e - ven say it glows.

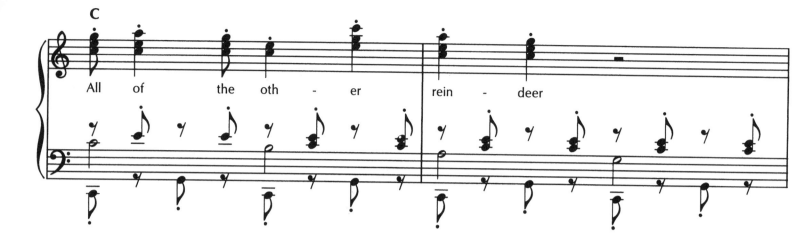

All of the oth - er rein - deer

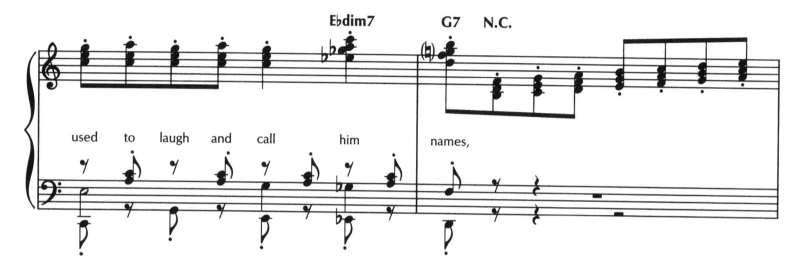

used to laugh and call him names,

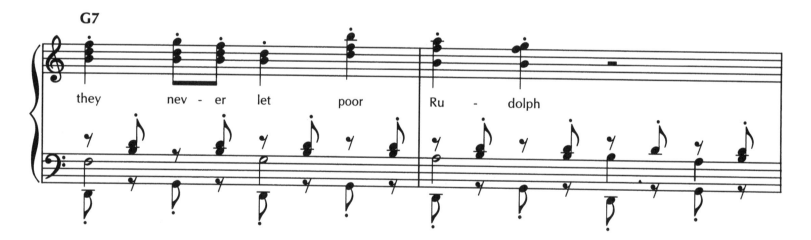

they nev - er let poor Ru - dolph

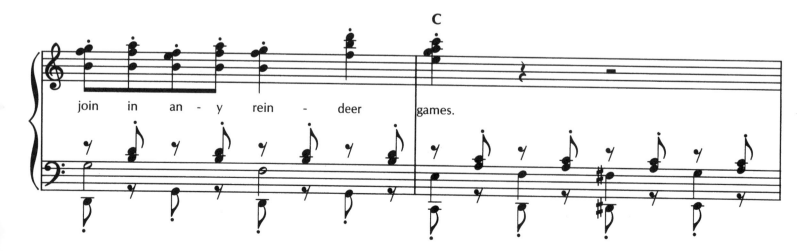

join in an - y rein - deer games.

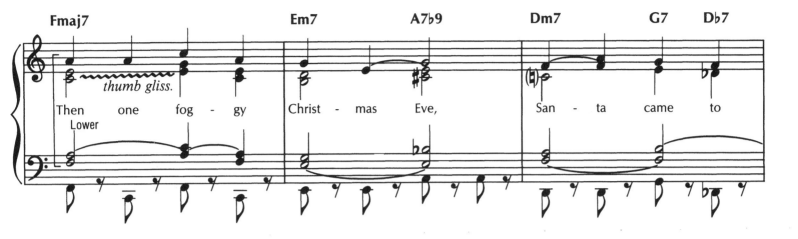

Then one fog-gy Christ - mas Eve, San - ta came to

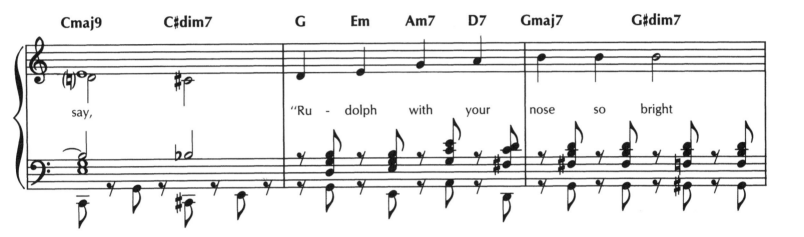

say, "Ru - dolph with your nose so bright

won't you guide my sleigh to - night?"—

Then how the rein - deer loved him,

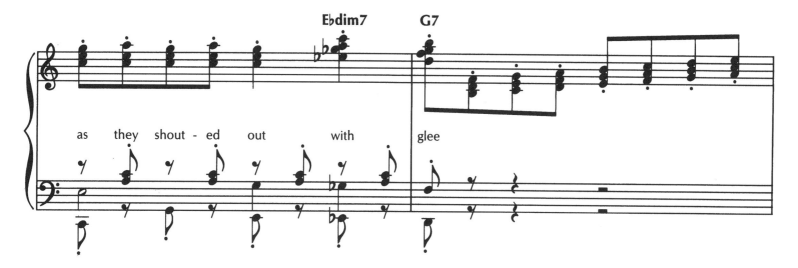

as they shout - ed out with glee

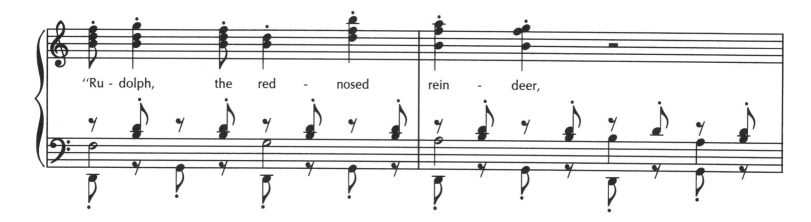

"Ru - dolph, the red - nosed rein - deer,

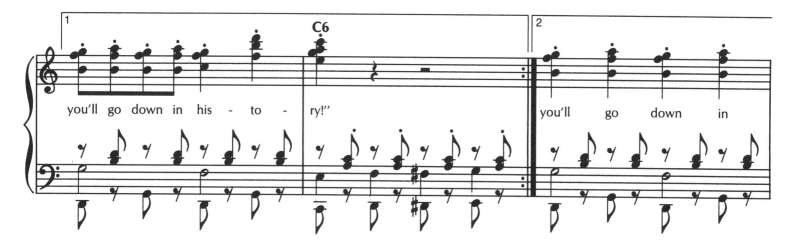

you'll go down in his - to - ry!" you'll go down in

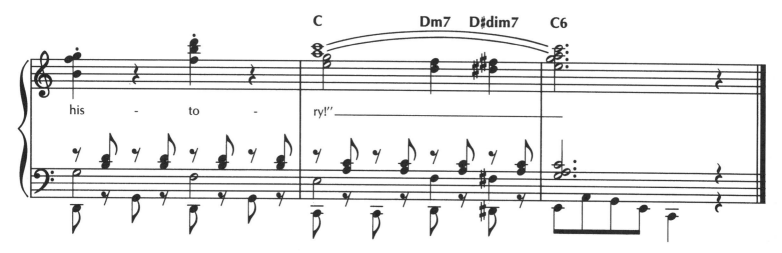

his - to - ry!"

See Amid the Winter's Snow

Registration 1

Words by Edward Caswall
Music by John Goss

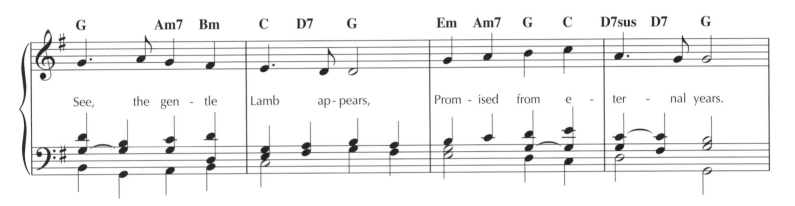

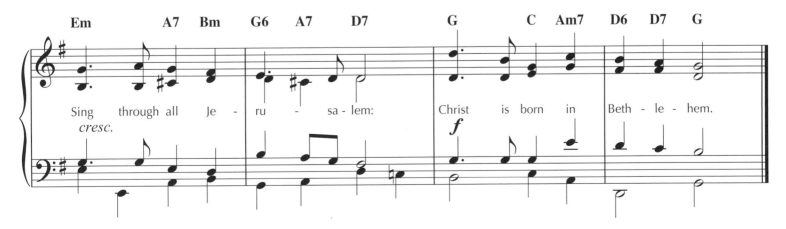

Shepherds, Shake Off Your Drowsy Sleep

Registration 8

Traditional French Carol

Brightly

Shep- herds, shake off your drow - sy sleep, rise and leave your sil - ly

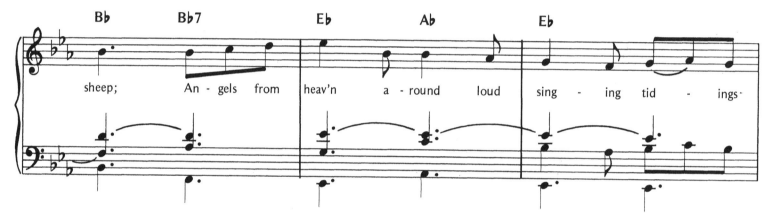

sheep; An - gels from heav'n a - round loud sing - ing tid - ings

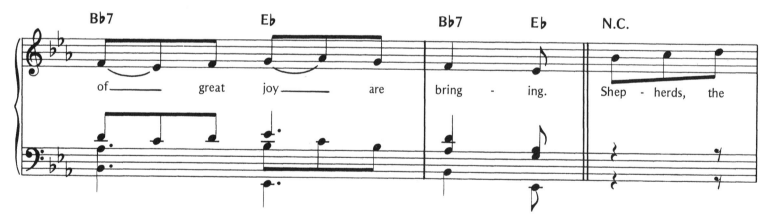

of ___ great joy ___ are bring - ing. Shep - herds, the

chor - us come and swell! Sing No - el, O sing ___ No - el!

Silver and Gold

Registration 48

Music and Lyrics by
Johnny Marks

Slowly, with expression

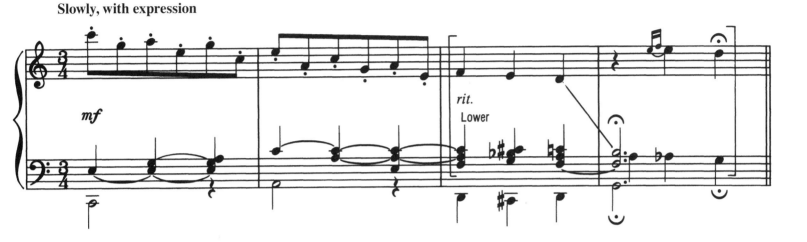

Sil - ver and gold, sil - ver and gold,

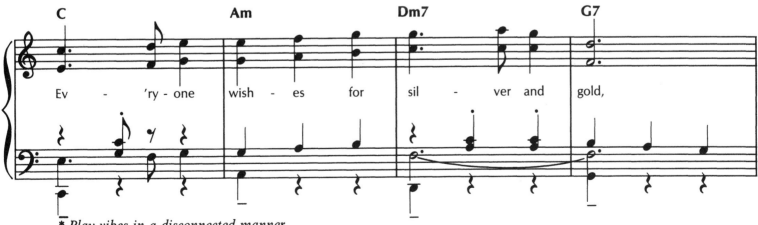

Ev - 'ry - one wish - es for sil - ver and gold,

* Play vibes in a disconnected manner.

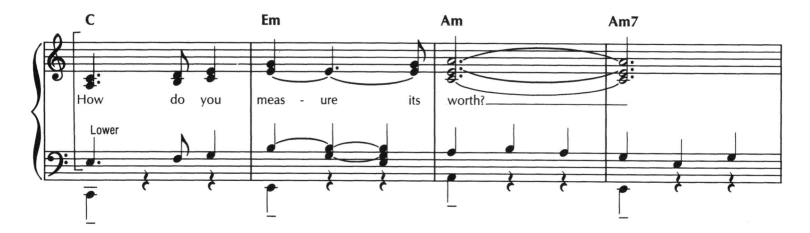

How do you meas - ure its worth? _____

Lower

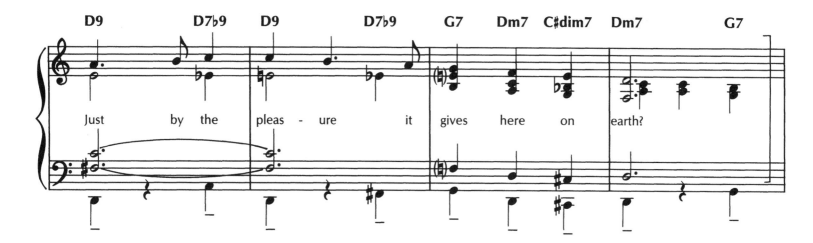

Just by the pleas - ure it gives here on earth?

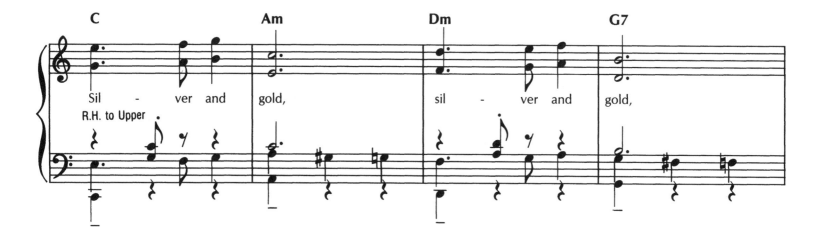

Sil - ver and gold, sil - ver and gold,

R.H. to Upper

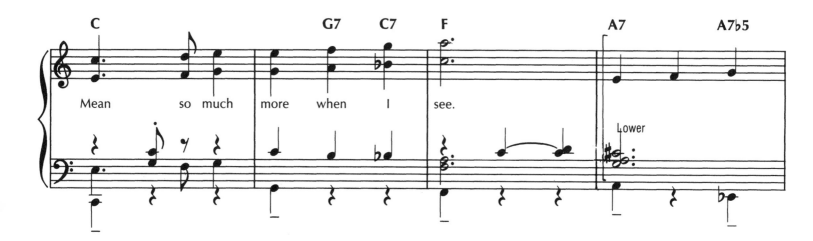

Mean so much more when I see.

Lower

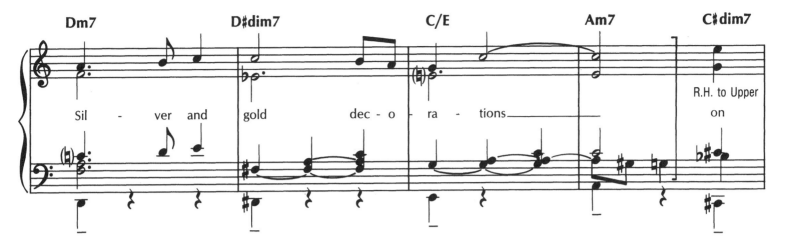

Sil - ver and gold dec - o - ra - tions

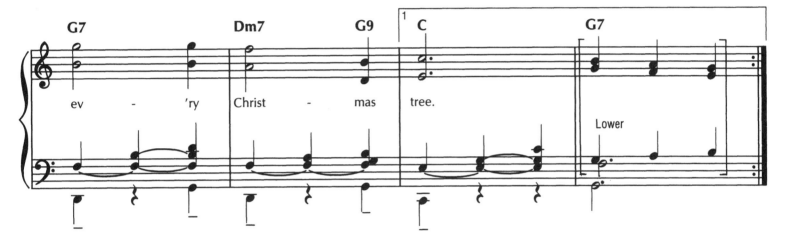

ev - 'ry Christ - mas tree.

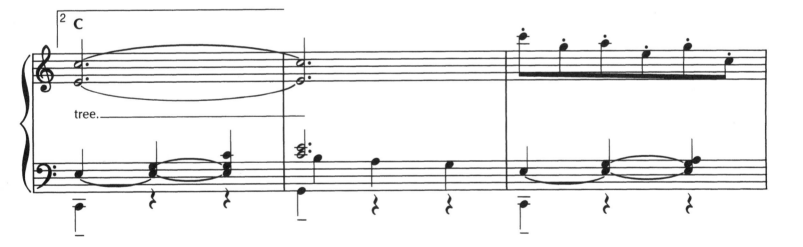

tree.

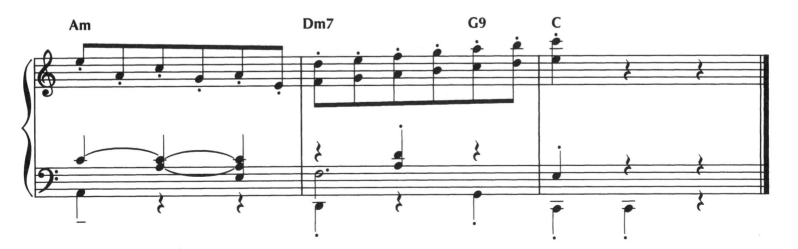

Silent Night

Registration 11

Words by Joseph Mohr
Translated by John F. Young
Music by Franz X. Gruber

Slowly, calmly

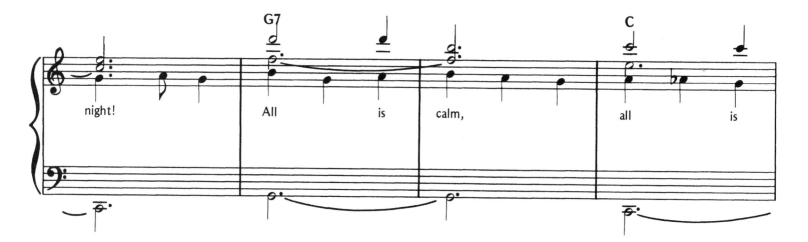

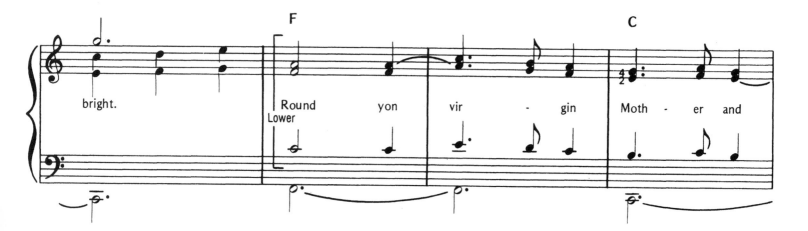

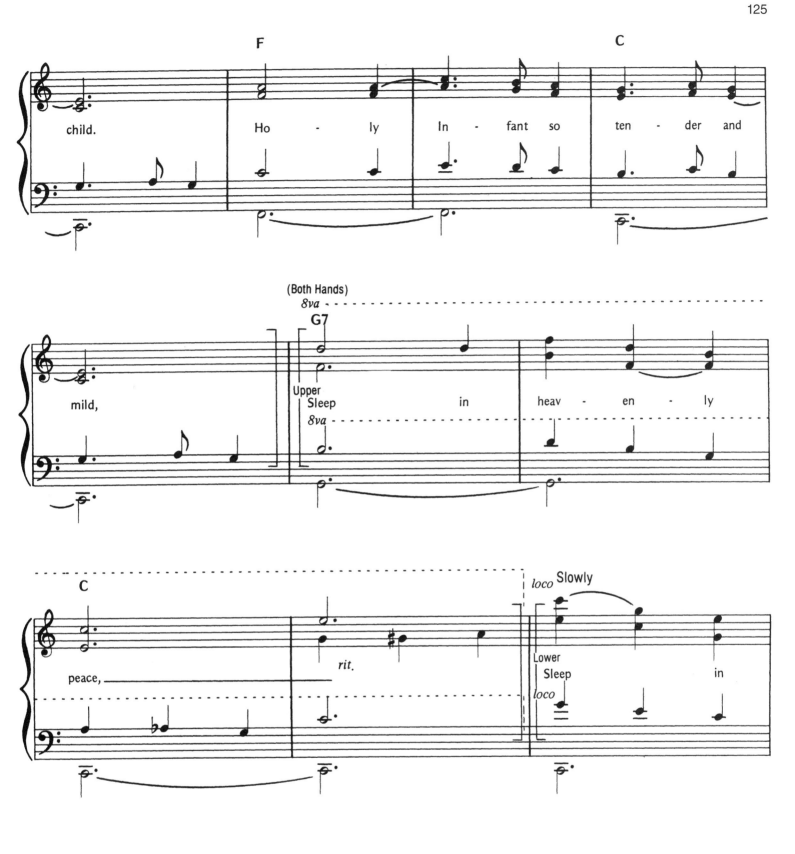

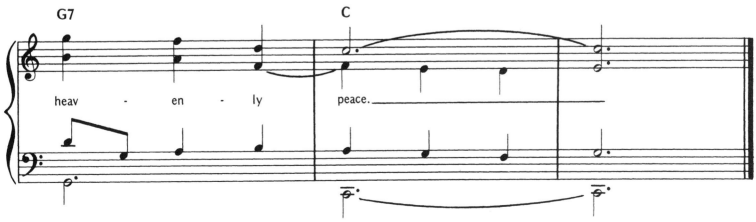

Silver Bells
from the Paramount Picture THE LEMON DROP KID

Registration 10

Words and Music by Jay Livingston
and Ray Evans

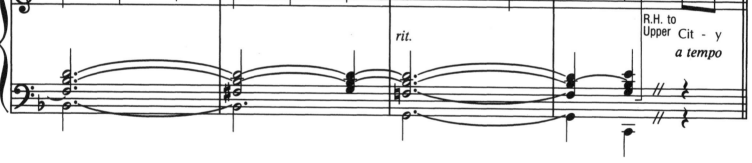

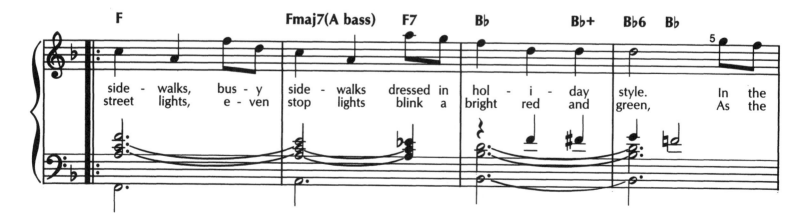

side - walks, bus - y
street lights, e - ven
side - walks dressed in
stop lights blink a
hol - i - day
bright red and
style.
green, In the
As the

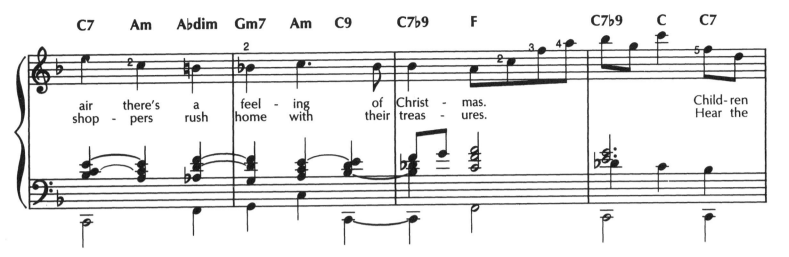

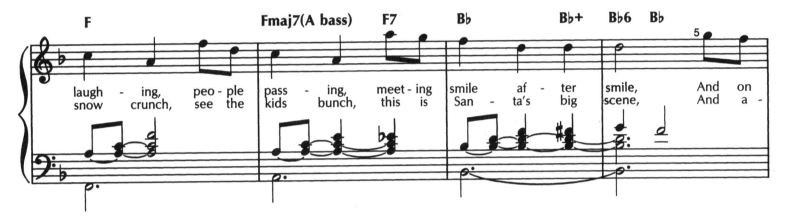

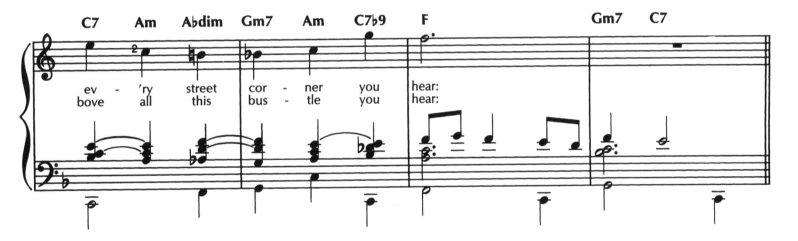

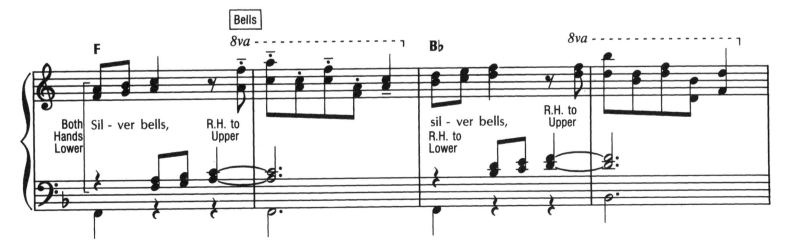

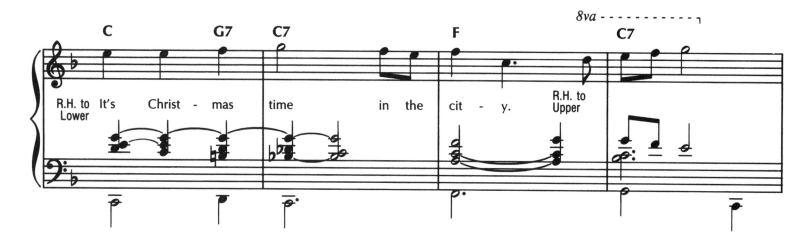

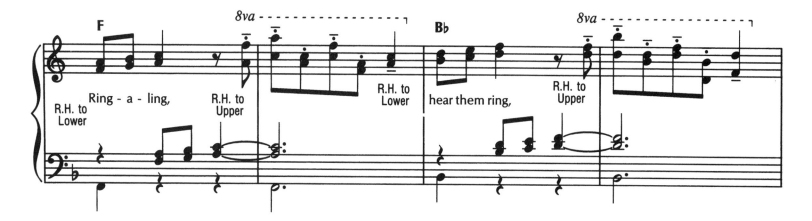

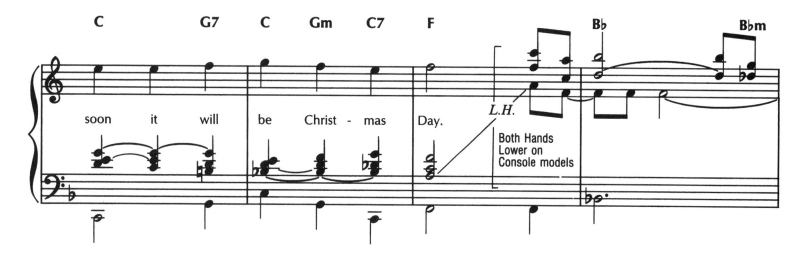

Sleep, O Sleep, My Lovely Child

Registration 3

Traditional Italian Carol

The Snow Lay on the Ground

Registration 15

Traditional Irish Carol

Moderately slow

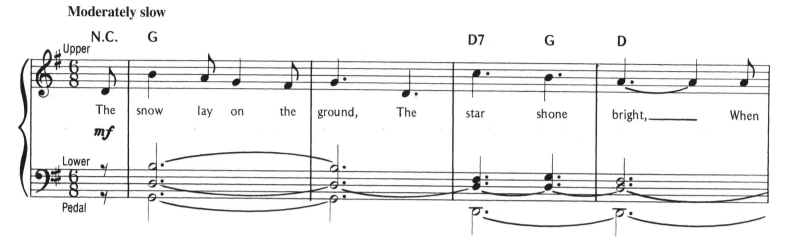

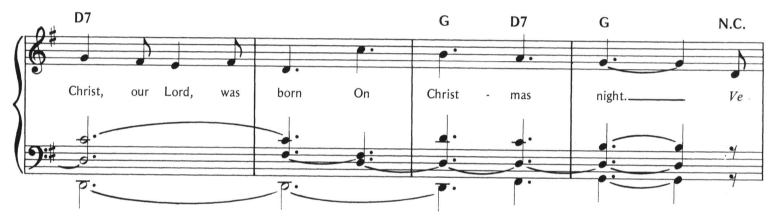

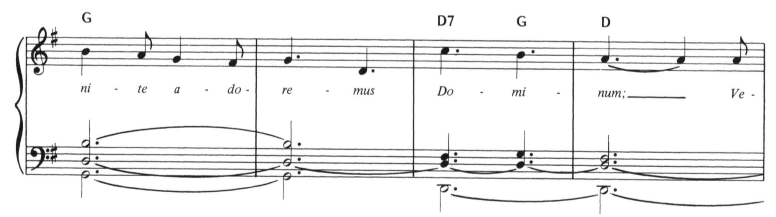

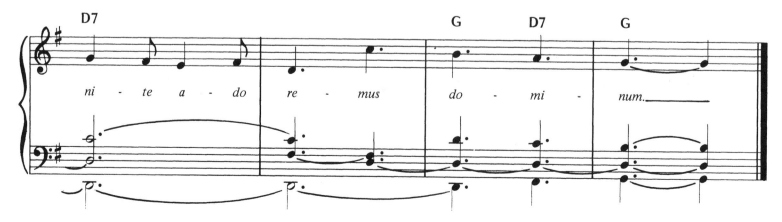

The Star Carol

Registration 31

Lyric by Wihla Hutson
Music by Alfred Burt

Suzy Snowflake

Registration 42

Words and Music by Sid Tepper
and Roy Bennett

*If you prefer the melody played simply, omit the
bottom notes of the melody in the "cute" 4 measures.
Fingering optional. Hold for full value.)

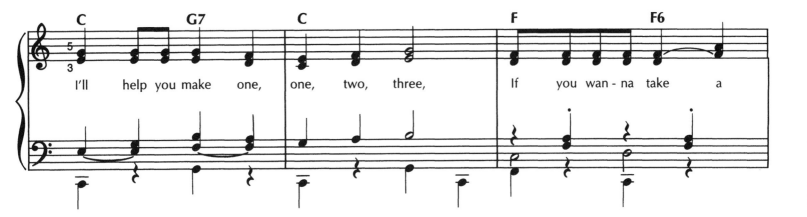

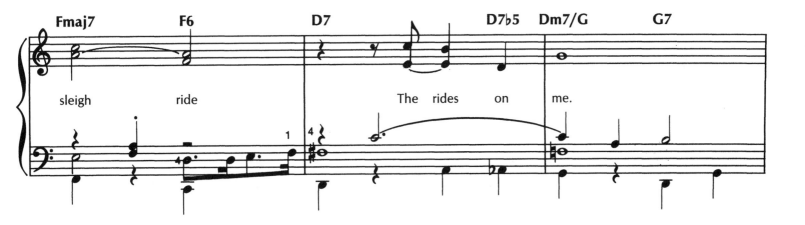

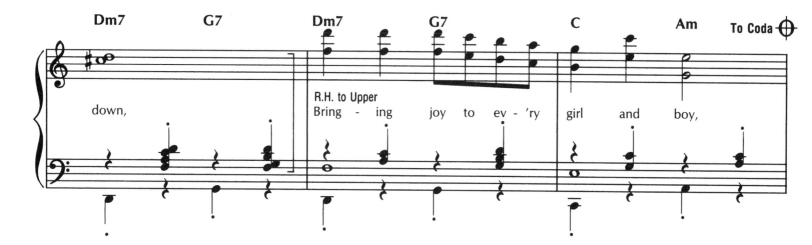

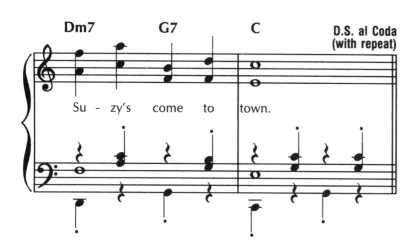

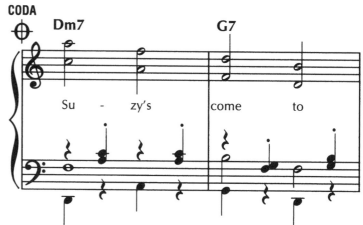

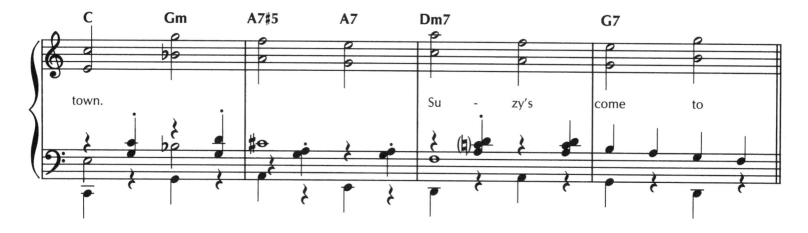

Up on the Housetop

Registration 11

Words and Music by
B.R. Hanby

Toyland
from BABES IN TOYLAND

Words by Glen MacDonough
Music by Victor Herbert

Registration 18

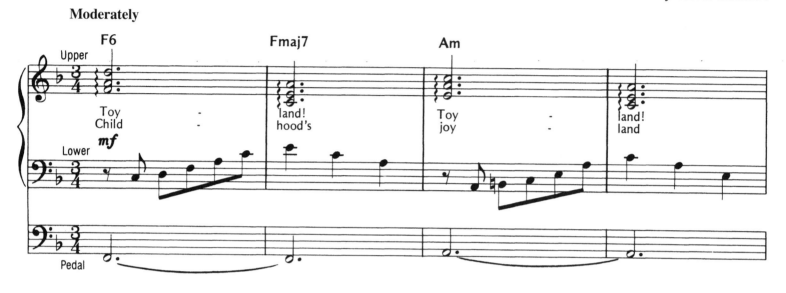

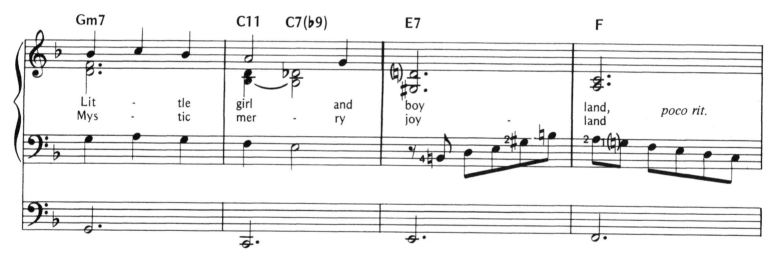

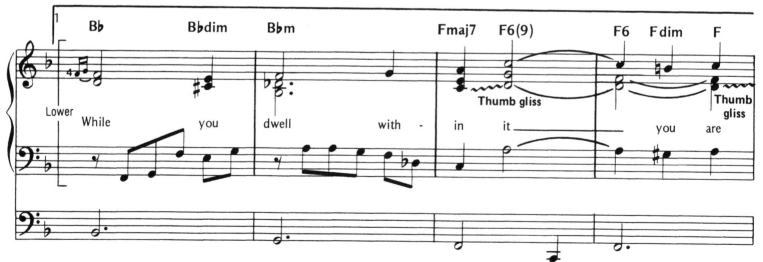

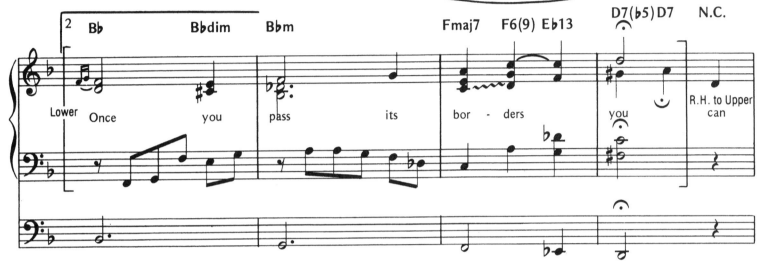

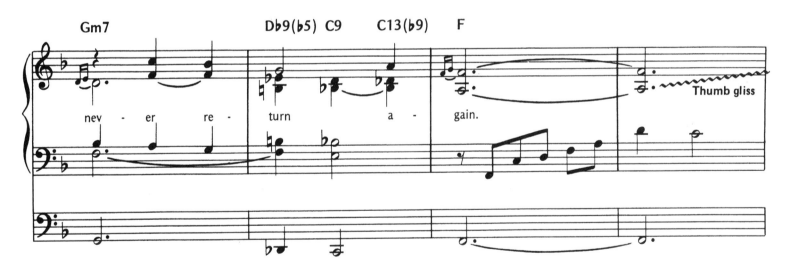

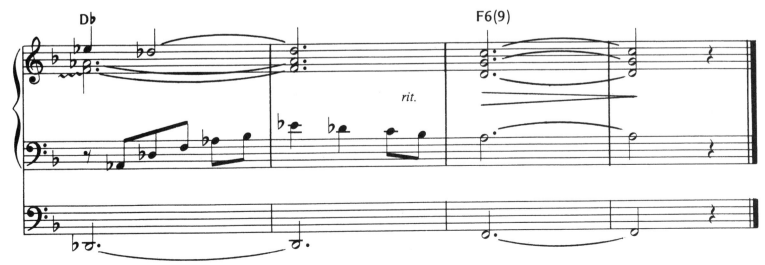

The Twelve Days of Christmas

Registration 8

Traditional English Carol

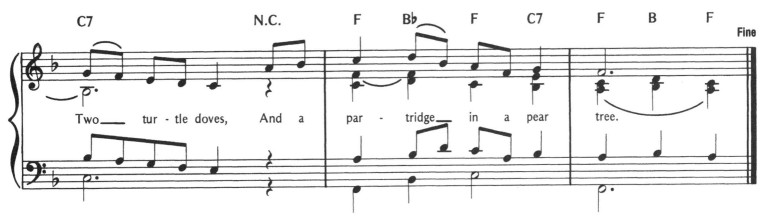

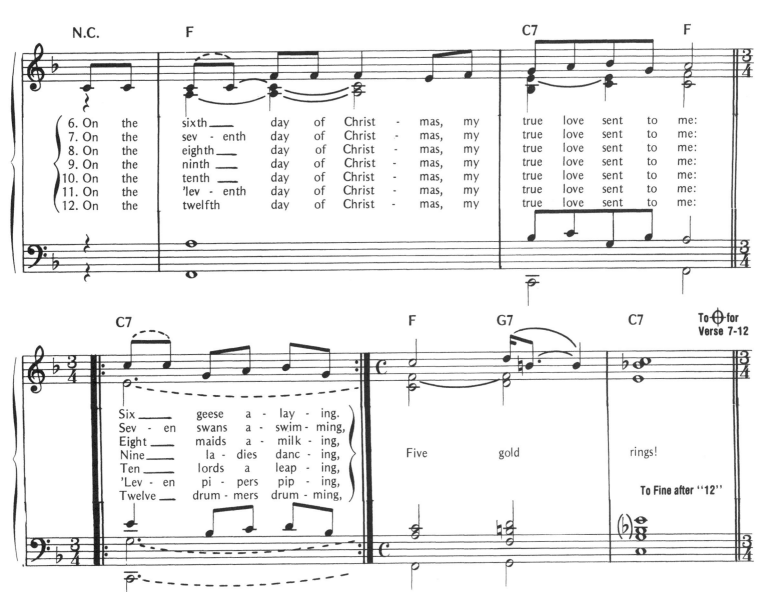

We Three Kings of Orient Are

Registration 4

Words and Music by
John H. Hopkins, Jr.

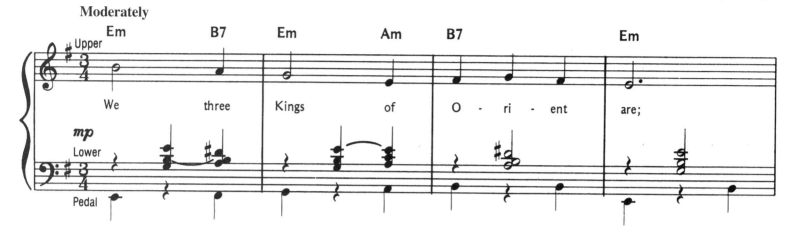

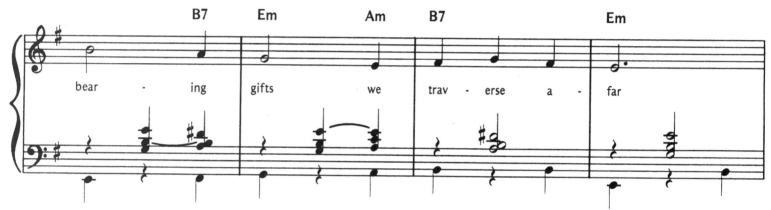

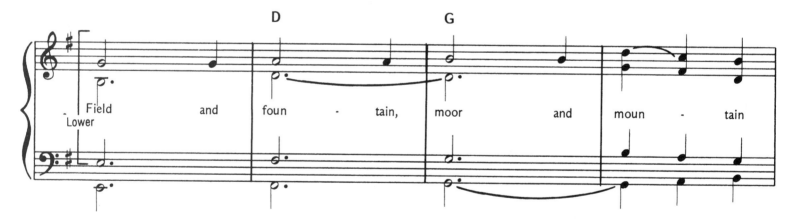

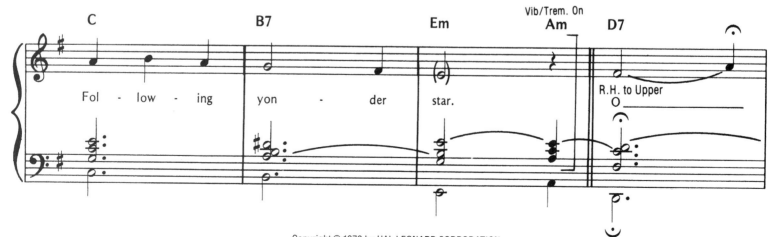

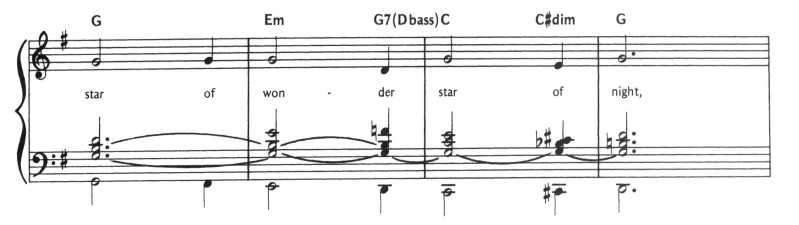

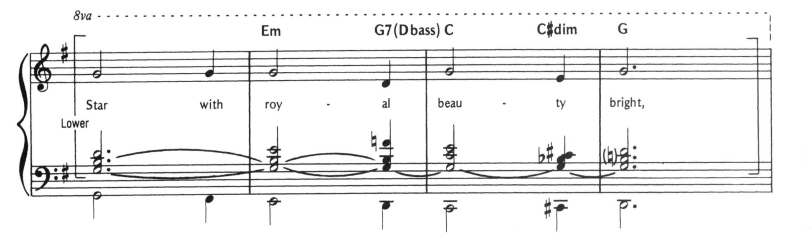

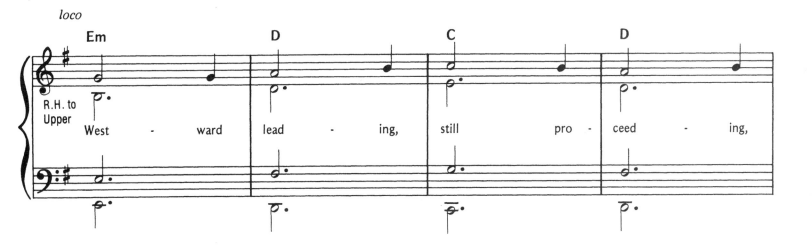

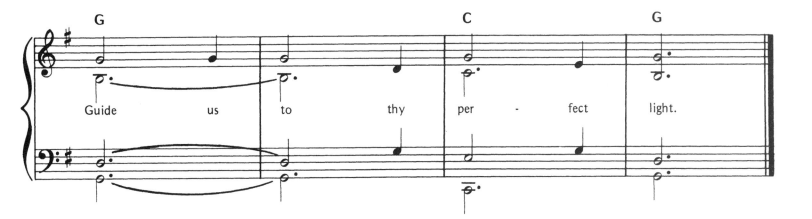

We Wish You a Merry Christmas

Registration 7

Traditional English Folksong

When Christ Was Born of Mary Free

Registration 15

Music by Arthur H. Brown
Traditional Text, 15th Century

What Child Is This?

Registration 12

Words by William C. Dix
16th Century English Melody

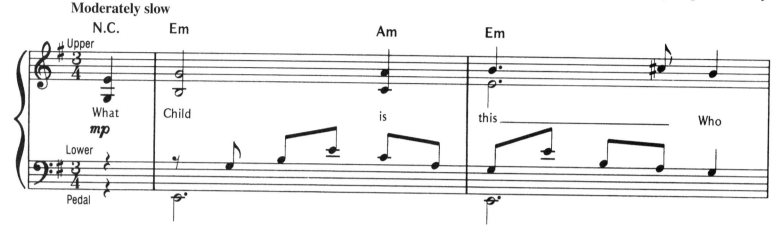

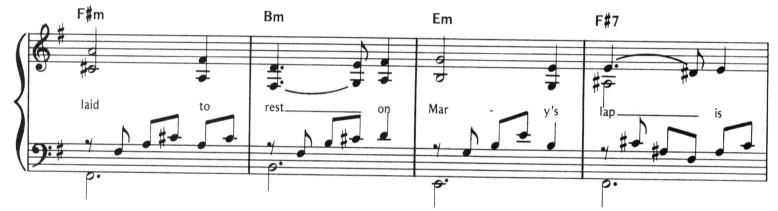

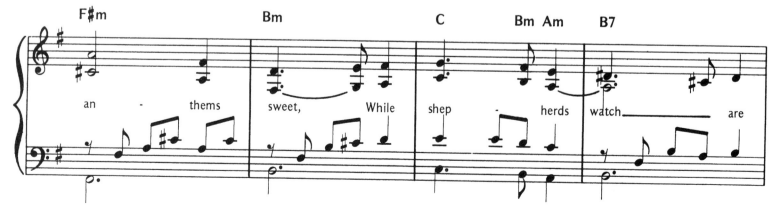

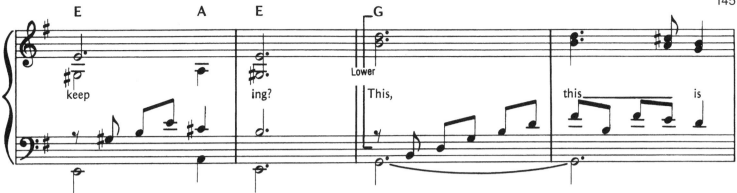

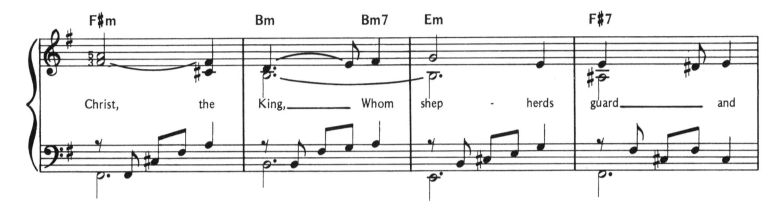

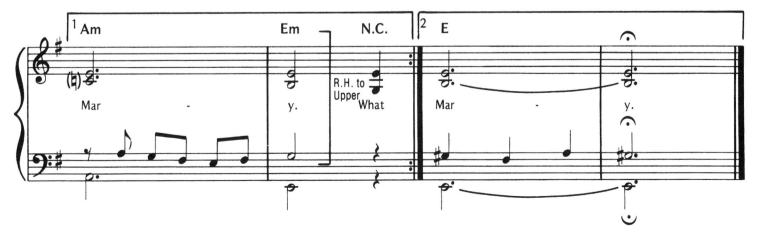

While Shepherds Watched Their Flocks

Registration 8

Words by Nahum Tate
Music by George Frideric Handel

Winter Wonderland

Registration 15

Words by Dick Smith
Music by Felix Bernard

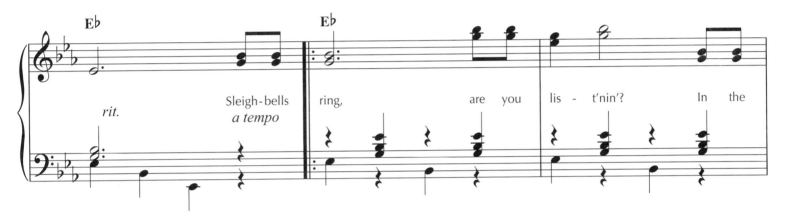

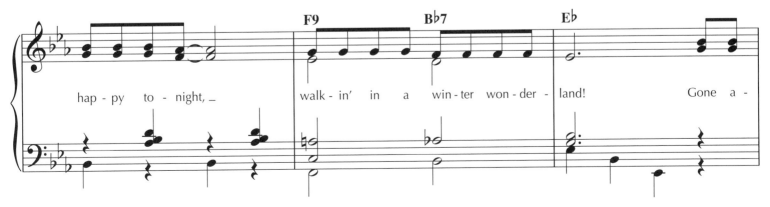

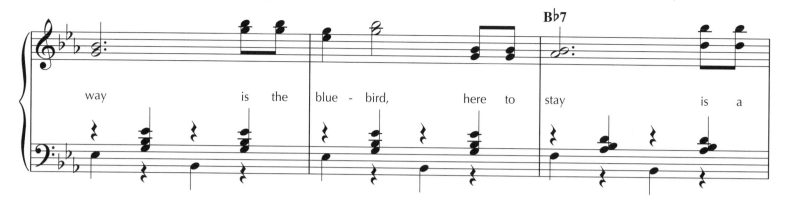

way   is the   blue - bird,   here to   stay   is a

new   bird;   {He   sings a   love   song ___   as   we   go   a - long, ___
                      {He's   sing - ing a   song ___   as   we   go   a - long, ___

walk - in'   in   a   win - ter won - der - land!   In   the   mead - ow   we   can   build   a
walk - in'   in   a   win - ter won - der - land!   In   the   mead - ow   we   can   build   a

Upper

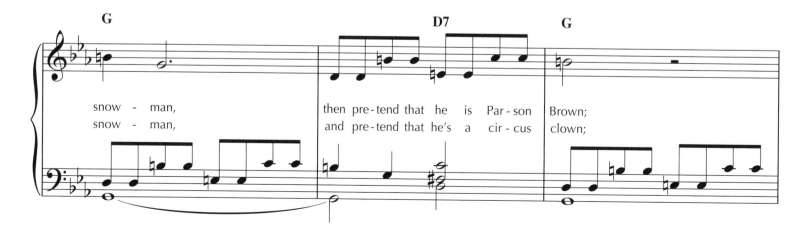

snow - man,   then pre - tend that he   is   Par - son   Brown;
snow - man,   and   pre - tend that he's a   cir - cus   clown;

He'll say, "Are you mar-ried?" We'll say, "No, man! But
We'll have lots of fun with Mis-ter Snow-man, un-

you can do the job when you're in
til the oth-er kid-dies knock 'im

town!" Later on, we'll con-a-spire, — as we dream by the
down! When it snows, ain't it thrill-in' though your nose gets a

fire, — to face un-a-fraid, — the plans that we made, —
chill-in'? We'll frol-ic and play the Es-ki-mo way, —

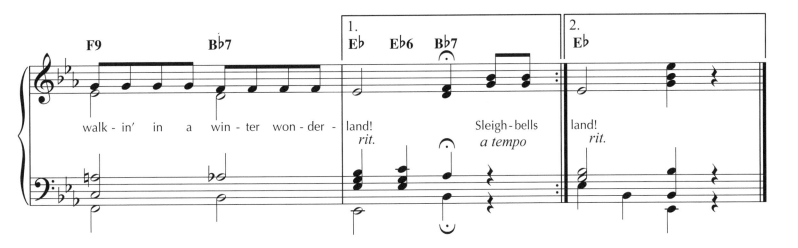

walk-in' in a win-ter won-der-land! Sleigh-bells land!

White Christmas
from the Motion Picture Irving Berlin's HOLIDAY INN

Registration 4

Words and Music by
Irving Berlin

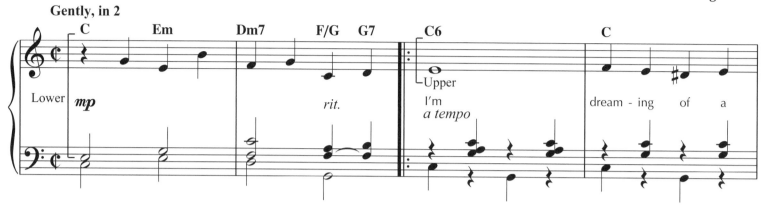

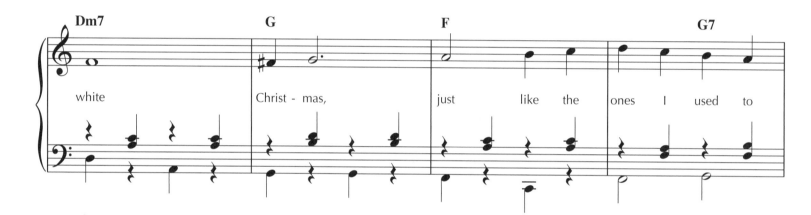

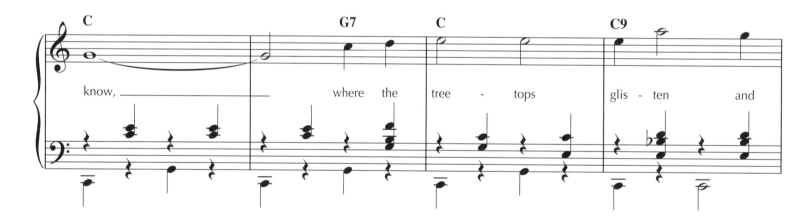

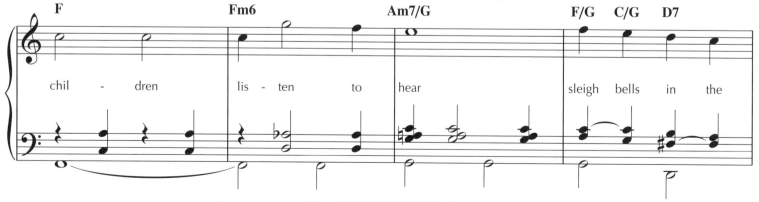

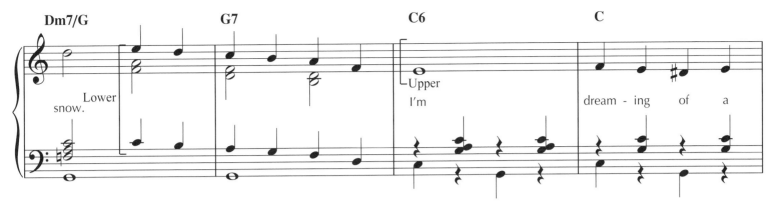

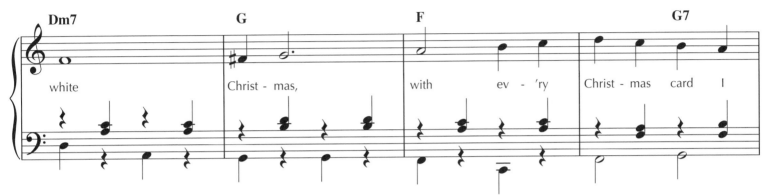

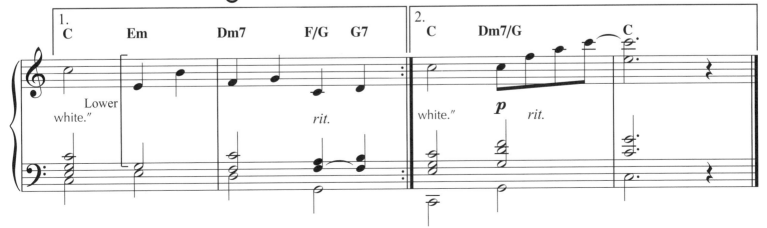

REGISTRATION CHART

Each numbered registration will produce a different sound. Match the number on the song to the same number on this chart; then engage the organ voices and controls as indicated.

ELECTRONIC ORGANS	DRAWBAR ORGANS	ELECTRONIC ORGANS	DRAWBAR ORGANS
1 Upper: Clarinet 8' Lower: Flute 8', String 4' Pedal: 16', 8' Medium Vib./Trem.: On, Full (Opt. Off)	Upper: 00 8282 805 Lower: (00) 6543 322 Pedal: 52 Vib./Trem.: On, Full (Opt. Off)	**13** Upper: Flutes (or Tibias) 8', 2', String 4', Reed 4' Lower: Diapason 8' (Flute 8', String 8') Pedal: 16', 8', Medium Vib./Trem.: Off	Upper: 00 8008 555 Lower: (00) 6554 222 Pedal: 54 Vib./Trem.: Off
2 Upper: Flutes (or Tibias) 8', 4', 2', 1' Lower: Flute 8', String 8' Pedal: 16', 8' Medium Vib./Trem.: On, Full (Opt. Off)	Upper: 00 8282 805 Lower: (00) 6543 322 Pedal: 52 Vib./Trem.: On, Full (Opt. Off)	**14** Upper: Flutes (or Tibias) 8', 4', 2', String 8' Lower: Diapason 8', Reeds 8', 4' Pedal: 16', 8' Medium Loud Vib./Trem.: Off	Upper: 00 8888 000 Lower: (00) 6655 554 Pedal: 55 Vib./Trem.: Off
3 Upper: Flutes (or Tibias) 8', 4' Lower: Flute 8', Reed 4' Pedal: 16', 8' Medium Soft Vib./Trem.: On, Small (Opt. Off)	Upper: 00 8008 000 Lower: (00) 6322 441 Pedal: 52 Vib./Trem.: On, Small (Opt. Off)	**15** Upper: Full Organ 16', 8', 4', 2', 1' Lower: Flutes 8', 4', 2', Strings 8', 4' Pedal: 16', 8 Medium Loud Vib./Trem.: On, Full (Opt. Off)	Upper: 60 6666 666 Lower: (00) 7746 554 Pedal: 62 Vib./Trem.: On, Full (Opt. Off)
4 Upper: Oboe (or Reed) 8' Lower: Flute 8', String 4' Pedal: 16', 8' Medium Soft Vib./Trem.: Upper: Off Lower: On	Upper: 00 4685 421 Lower: (00) 5433 321 Pedal: 52 Vib./Trem.: Upper: Off Lower: On	**16** Upper: Flutes (or Tibias) 8', 1', Reed 4' (Tierce) Lower: Flute 8', String 4' Pedal: 16', 8' Medium Vib./Trem.: Off	Upper: 00 8000 468 Lower: (00) 6322 222 Pedal: 54 Vib./Trem.: Off
5 Upper: Trumpet (or Brass) 8' Lower: Diapason 8' Pedal: 16', 8' Medium Vib./Trem.: On, Small (Opt. Off)	Upper: 00 6787 654 Lower: (00) 6543 221 Pedal: 53 Vib./Trem.: On, Small (Opt. Off)	**17** Upper: Flute (or Tibia) 16' (or Bassoon 16') Reed 8', String 4' Lower: Flutes 8', 4', String 8' Pedal: 16', 8' Medium Loud Vib./Trem.: On, Full (Opt. Off)	Upper: 88 0080 660 Lower: (00) 7755 422 Pedal: 65 Vib./Trem.: On, Full (Opt. Off)
6 Upper: String 8' Lower: Flute 8', Reed 4' Pedal: 16', 8' Medium Soft Vib./Trem.: On, Full (Opt. Off)	Upper: 00 4456 667 Lower: (00) 6332 221 Pedal: 52 Vib./Trem.: On, Full (Opt. Off)	**18** Upper: Flutes (or Tibias) 8', 4', 2', Reed 4' Lower: Flutes 8', 4', Horn 8' Pedal: 16', 8' Medium Vib./Trem.: On, Full	Upper: 00 8808 050 Lower: (00) 8880 000 Pedal: 62 Vib./Trem.: On, Full
7 Upper: Full Organ 16', 8', 4', 2', 1' Lower: Flutes 8', 4', String 8', Reed 4' Pedal: 16', 8' Medium Loud Vib./Trem.: On, Full (Opt. Off)	Upper: 60 8838 667 Lower: (00) 7654 332 Pedal: 65 Vib./Trem.: On, Full (Opt. Off)	**19** Upper: Full Organ 16', 8', 4', 2', 1' (Brilliant) Lower: Flutes 8', 4' Strings 8', 4', Reed 4' Pedal: 16', 8' Medium Loud/Sustain Vib./Trem.: On, Full	Upper: 60 8080 887 Lower: (00) 7754 443 Pedal: 56 String Bass Vib./Trem.: On, Full
8 Upper: Full Organ 8', 4', 2', 1' Lower: Flute 8', String 4', Reed 4' Pedal: 16', 8' Medium Vib./Trem.: On, Full (Opt. Off)	Upper: 00 8558 446 Lower: (00) 6644 232 Pedal: 55 Vib./Trem.: On, Full (Opt. Off)	**20** Upper: Full Organ 16', 8', 4', 2', 1' (Use Strings 8', 4') Lower: Diapason 8', Flutes 8', 4', 2', String 8', Reed 4' Pedal: 16', 8' Medium Loud/Sustain Vib./Trem.: On, Full	Upper: 60 8586 666 Lower: (00) 7764 443 Pedal: 56 String Bass Vib./Trem.: On, Full
9 Upper: Flutes (or Tibias) 16', 8', 4', 2', 1' Lower: Diapason 8', Flute 8', String 8' Pedal: 16', 8' Medium Vib./Trem.: On, Small (Opt. Off)	Upper: 60 8808 008 Lower: (00) 6656 543 Pedal: 54 Vib./Trem.: On, Small (Opt. Off)	**21** Upper: Flutes (or Tibias) 16', 8', 5⅓', 4' Lower: Diapason 8', Flute 4', String 8' Pedal: 16', 8', Sustain (Add Percussive Edge) Vib./Trem.: On, Full Auto Rhythm: Rock	Upper: 44 8855 000 Lower: (00) 7753 221 Pedal: 48 Sustain Vib./Trem.: On, Full Auto Rhythm: Rock
10 Upper: Flute (or Tibia) 8', Horn 4', String 4' Lower: Flutes 8', 4' Pedal: 16', 8' Medium Vib./Trem.: Off	Upper: 00 8880 080 Lower: (00) 8800 000 Pedal: 54 Vib./Trem.: Off	**22** Upper: Full Organ 16', 8', 4', 2', 1' Lower: Flutes 8', 4', Strings 8', 4' Pedal: 16', 8', Sustain Vib./Trem.: On, Full Auto Rhythm: Rock	Upper: 70 8807 544 Lower: (00) 7653 221 Pedal: 48 Sustain Vib./Trem.: On, Full Auto Rhythm: Rock
11 Upper: Flutes (or Tibias) 16', 4', Horn 8' Lower: Diapason 8', String 8' Pedal: 16', 8' Medium Vib./Trem.: On, Full (Opt. Off)	Upper: 80 0800 805 Lower: (00) 6554 221 Pedal: 54 Vib./Trem.: On, Full (Opt. Off)	**23** Upper: Saxophone 8' (Reed 8') Lower: Flutes 8', 4', String 8' Pedal: 8' Sustain Vib./Trem.: On, Full Auto Rhythm: Rock	Upper: 00 8808 466 Lower: (00) 8644 223 Pedal: 48 Sustain Vib./Trem.: On, Full Auto Rhythm: Rock
12 Upper: Flutes (or Tibias) 8', 4', 2' Lower: Clarinet 8' (or flute 8', Reed 4') Pedal: 16', 8' Medium Vib./Trem.: Off	Upper: 00 8808 000 Lower: (00) 8080 400 Pedal: 52 Vib./Trem.: Off	**24** Upper: Piano (Flutes or Tibias 8', 2') Lower: Flute 8', String 8' Pedal: 16', 8' Sustain Vib./Trem.: On, Full Auto Rhythm: Rock	Upper: Piano 00 8008 000 Lower: (00) 8421 000 Pedal: 48 Sustain Vib./Trem.: On, Full Auto Rhythm: Rock

ELECTRONIC ORGANS	DRAWBAR ORGANS	ELECTRONIC ORGANS	DRAWBAR ORGANS
25 Upper: Clarinet 8', 　　　Flute (or Tibia) 4' Lower: Flute 8', Soft Strings 8', 4' Pedal: 16', 8' Sustain Vib./Trem.: On, Full Auto Rhythm: Ballad or Swing	Upper:　00　8883 804 Lower: (00) 7653 222 Pedal:　58 Sustain Vib./Trem.: On, Full Auto Rhythm: Ballad or Swing	**39** Upper: Flutes (or Tibias) 8', 4' 　　　Reed 8' Lower: Flutes and Strings 8', 4' Pedal: 16', 8', Sustain Vib./Trem.: On Full Auto Rhythm: Rock	Upper:　30　8448 621 Lower: (00) 8642 110 Pedal:　47 Sustain Vib./Trem.: On, Full Auto Rhythm: Rock
26 Upper: Flutes (or Tibias) 16', 8', 　　　4', 2' Lower: Flute 8', Reed 8' Pedal: 16', 8' Sustain Vib./Trem.: On, Full Auto Rhythm: Ballad or Swing	Upper:　40　8808 008 Lower: (00) 7754 433 Pedal:　57 Sustain Vib./Trem.: On, Full Auto Rhythm: Ballad or Swing	**40** Upper: Saxophone (Reed) 8' Lower: Flutes 8', 4', String 8' Pedal: 16', 8' Sustain Vib./Trem.: On, Full Auto Rhythm: Ballad	Upper:　00　8880 000 Lower: (00) 7333 344 Pedal:　47 Sustain Vib./Trem.: On, Full Auto Rhythm: Ballad
27 Upper: Flutes (or Tibias) 8', 4', 2' 　　　Trumpet 8' Lower: Flutes 8', 4, String 8' Pedal: 16', 8' Sustain Vib./Trem.: On, Full Auto Rhythm: Ballad or Swing	Upper:　00　8408 005 Lower: (00) 8463 323 Pedal:　57 Sustain Vib./Trem.: On, Full Auto Rhythm: Ballad or Swing	**41** Upper: Strings 8', 4' Lower: Flutes 8', 4', 2', Reed 8' Pedal: 16', 8' Sustain Vib./Trem.: On, Full Auto Rhythm: Waltz	Upper:　00　4458 888 Lower: (00) 7336 444 Pedal:　64 Sustain Vib./Trem.: On, Full Auto Rhythm: Waltz
28 Upper: Flutes (or Tibias) 8', 2' 　　　Reed (Sax) Lower: Flutes 8', 4', Strings 8', 4' Pedal: 16', 8' Sustain Vib./Trem.: On, Full Auto Rhythm: Jazz Rock or Swing	Upper:　00　8086 643 Lower: (00) 6833 222 Pedal:　46 Sustain Vib./Trem.: On, Full Auto Rhythm: Jazz Rock or Swing	**42** Upper: Vibraphone (Sustain) Lower: Diapason 8', Flute 8' 　　　String 8' Pedal: 16', 8' Sustain Vib./Trem.: On, Full Auto Rhythm: Ballad or Jazz Rock	Upper: Vibraphone (Sustain) Lower: (00) 7654 322 Pedal:　47 Sustain Vib./Trem.: On, Full Auto Rhythm: Ballad or Jazz Rock
29 Upper: Flutes (or Tibias) 16', 8', 4', 　　　2', 1' Lower: Diapason 8', Flutes 8', 4' 　　　String 8' Pedal: 16', 8' Sustain Vib./Trem.: On, Full Auto Rhythm: Swing	Upper:　60　8808 008 Lower: (00) 8304 444 Pedal:　57 Sustain Vib./Trem.: On, Full Auto Rhythm: Swing	**43** Upper: Trombone 8' (Reed 8') Lower: Flutes and Strings 8', 4' Pedal: 16', 8' Sustain Vib./Trem.: On, Full Auto Rhythm: Swing	Upper:　00　8880 800 Lower: (00) 7444 433 Pedal:　46 Sustain Vib./Trem.: On, Full Auto Rhythm: Swing
30 Upper: Flutes (or Tibias) 8', 4' 　　　String 4' Lower: Flutes 8', 2', String 8' Pedal: 16', 8' Sustain Vib./Trem.: On, Full Auto Rhythm: Ballad or Swing	Upper:　00　8800 804 Lower: (00) 7003 333 Pedal:　47 Sustain Vib./Trem.: On, Full Auto Rhythm: Ballad or Swing	**44** Upper: Flutes (or Tibias) 8', 4', 2' 　　　Trumpet 8' Lower: Flutes 8', 4', String 8' Pedal: 16', 8' Sustain Vib./Trem.: On, Full Auto Rhythm: Ballad or Swing	Upper:　00　8408 005 Lower: (00) 8463 323 Pedal:　57 Sustain Vib./Trem.: On, Full Auto Rhythm: Ballad or Swing
31 Upper: Flutes (or Tibias) 4', 2' 　　　Oboe 8' Lower: Flutes 8', 4', String 8' Pedal: 16', 8' Sustain Vib./Trem.: On, Full	Upper:　00　6804 720 Lower: (00) 8522 100 Pedal:　54 Sustain Vib./Trem.: On, Full	**45** Upper: Flutes (or Tibias) 8', 2' Lower: Flute 8', Reed 8' Pedal: 16', 8' Sustain Vib./Trem.: On, Full Auto Rhythm: Waltz	Upper:　00　8408 004 Lower: (00) 8532 220 Pedal:　47 Sustain Vib./Trem.: On, Full Auto Rhythm: Waltz
32 Upper: Flutes (or Tibias) 8', 4', 2' 　　　String 8' Lower: Diapason 8', Flute 8' 　　　Reed 8' Pedal: 16', 8' Sustain Vib./Trem.: On, Full Auto Rhythm: Rock	Upper:　00　8808 008 Lower: (00) 7432 100 Pedal:　48 Sustain Vib./Trem.: On, Full Auto Rhythm: Rock	**46** Upper: Flutes (or Tibias) 8', 4', 2' Lower: Flutes 8', 4', Strings 8', 4' Pedal: 16', 8' Sustain Vib./Trem.: On, Full Auto Rhythm: Ballad	Upper:　00　8808 008 Lower: (00) 8543 331 Pedal:　47 Sustain Vib./Trem.: On, Full Auto Rhythm: Ballad
33 Upper: Full Organ 16', 8', 4', 2' Lower: Flutes 8', 4', Strings 8', 4' 　　　Reed 4' Pedal: 16', 8' Sustain Vib./Trem.: On, Full Auto Rhythm: Ballad	Upper:　80　4808 877 Lower: (00) 8634 210 Pedal:　48 Sustain Vib./Trem.: On, Full Auto Rhythm: Ballad	**47** Upper: Flutes (or Tibias) 8', 2' Lower: Flutes 8', 4', Strings 8', 4' Pedal: 16', 8', Sustain Vib./Trem.: On, Full Auto Rhythm: Swing or Jazz Rock	Upper:　00　8008 880 Lower: (00) 8764 321 Pedal:　57 Sustain Vib./Trem.: On, Full Auto Rhythm: Swing or Jazz Rock
34 Upper: Flutes (or Tibias) 16', 4', 2' Lower: Diapason 8', Flute 8' 　　　String 4' Pedal: 16', 8' Sustain Vib./Trem.: On, Full Auto Rhythm: Waltz	Upper:　70　8080 807 Lower: (00) 8624 310 Pedal:　48 Sustain Vib./Trem.: On, Full Auto Rhythm: Waltz	**48** Upper: Vibraphone (Sustain) Lower: Flutes and Strings 8', 4' Pedal: 16', 8', Sustain Vib./Trem.: On, Full Auto Rhythm: Waltz	Upper:　00　8008 000 (Sustain) Lower: (00) 7434 321 Pedal:　56 Sustain Vib./Trem.: Upper-Off, Lower-On Auto Rhythm: Waltz
35 Upper: Trumpet 8' Lower: Flutes 8', 4', String 8' Pedal: 16', 8' Sustain Vib./Trem.: On, Full Auto Rhythm: 4/4 March	Upper:　00　5688 754 Lower: (00) 7654 222 Pedal:　47 Sustain Vib./Trem.: On, Full Auto Rhythm: 4/4 March	**49** Upper: Flutes (or Tibias) 8', 4' 　　　String 8' Lower: Flutes 8', 2⅔', String 8' Pedal: 16', 8' Sustain Vib./Trem.: On, Full Auto Rhythm: Swing	Upper:　00　8880 000 Lower: (00) 7654 322 Pedal:　47 Sustain Vib./Trem.: On, Full Vib./Trem.: Swing
36 Upper: Flutes (or Tibias) 8', 4', 　　　Piano 8' Lower: Diapason 8', String 8' Pedal: 16', 8' Sustain Vib./Trem.: On, Full Auto Rhythm: Waltz	Upper:　00　8008 000, Piano Lower: (00) 7744 333 Pedal:　37 Sustain Vib./Trem.: On, Full Auto Rhythm: Waltz	**50** Upper: Flutes (or Tibias) 16', 8', 4', 2⅔' 　　　Strings 8' Lower: Flute 8', String 4', Reed 8' Pedal: 16', 8' Sustain Vib./Trem.: On, Full Auto Rhythm: Rock	Upper:　60　8888 000 Lower: (00) 8544 332 Pedal:　48 Sustain Vib./Trem.: On, Full Auto Rhythm: Rock
37 Upper: Chime Lower: Flutes 8', 4', String 4' Pedal: 16', Sustain Vib./Trem.: On, Full (Small For 　　　Liturgical)	Upper: Chime Lower: (00) 7004 033 Pedal:　63 Sustain Vib./Trem.: On, Full	**51** Upper: Reed or Saxophone 16' 　　　Flute 5⅓' Lower: Flutes 8', 4', String 8' Pedal: 16', 8' Sustain Vib./Trem.: On, Full Auto Rhythm: Waltz	Upper:　88　8085 343 Lower: (00) 8624 232 Pedal:　68 Sustain Vib./Trem.: On, Full Auto Rhythm: Waltz
38 Upper: Flutes (or Tibias) 8', 2', 　　　Harpsichord Lower: Flutes 8', 4', Strings 8' Pedal: 16', 8' Sustain Vib./Trem.: On, Full Auto Rhythm: Swing	Upper:　00　8008 008 　　　(add Harpsichord) Lower: (00) 7654 322 Pedal:　46 Sustain Vib./Trem.: On, Full Auto Rhythm: Swing	**52** Upper: Flutes (or Tibias) 16', 8', 　　　5⅓', String 8' Lower: Diapason 8', Flute 8', Reed 8' Pedal: 16', 8' Sustain Vib./Trem.: On, Full Auto Rhythm: Ballad or Swing	Upper:　88　8060 600 Lower: (00) 8654 322 Pedal:　67 Sustain Vib./Trem.: On, Full Auto Rhythm: Ballad or Swing

GREAT ORGAN SELECTIONS

BIG BAND & SWING
Relive the dance hall days with this great collection of 25 swingin' favorites: All or Nothing at All • Ballin' the Jack • Basin Street Blues • East of the Sun • I Can't Get Started with You • I'm Beginning to See the Light • Manhattan • Mood Indigo • Old Devil Moon • Paper Doll • Route 66 • Sentimental Journey • Stormy Weather • Tenderly • Witchcraft • and more.
00199010 Organ $9.95

CHRISTMAS FAVORITES
80 Christmas classics every organist should know: Auld Lang Syne • Away in a Manger • Blue Christmas • Christmas Time Is Here • Dance of the Sugar Plum Fairy • The First Noël • Frosty the Snow Man • God Rest Ye Merry, Gentlemen • Have Yourself a Merry Little Christmas • I Saw Three Ships • It Came upon the Midnight Clear • Jingle Bells • Joy to the World • A Marshmallow World • O Holy Night • Rockin' Around the Christmas Tree • Silent Night • Up on the Housetop • What Child Is This? • White Christmas • and many more.
00144576 $14.99

CONTEMPORARY CHRISTIAN CLASSICS
12 songs of praise, including: El Shaddai • How Majestic Is Your Name • More Than Wonderful • Upon This Rock • We Shall Behold Him.
00199095 $6.95

GOSPEL TREASURES
35 gospel favorites for organ: Amazing Grace • Blessed Assurance • Higher Ground • I Love to Tell the Story • In the Garden • Just a Closer Walk with Thee • Nearer, My God, to Thee • The Old Rugged Cross • Rock of Ages • Shall We Gather at the River? • Sweet By and By • What a Friend We Have in Jesus • Wonderful Peace • and many more.
00144550 $7.99

LES MISÉRABLES
14 songs from Broadway's longest-running musical arranged for organ, including: At the End of the Day • Bring Him Home • Castle on a Cloud • Do You Hear the People Sing? • I Dreamed a Dream • In My Life • On My Own • and more.
00290270 $12.99

THE MOST BEAUTIFUL SONGS EVER
70 beautiful melodies arranged for organ: Autumn Leaves • Edelweiss • How High the Moon • If I Were a Bell • Luck Be a Lady • Misty • Ol' Man River • Satin Doll • Smile • Stardust • Summertime • Till There Was You • Unchained Melody • The Way You Look Tonight • Witchcraft • and more.
00144638 $16.99

105 FAVORITE HYMNS
HAL LEONARD ORGAN ADVENTURE SERIES – No. 18
arr. Bill Irwin
105 songs, including: Amazing Grace • The Church in the Wildwood • Holy, Holy, Holy • and more.
00212500 $10.95

THE PHANTOM OF THE OPERA
Nine songs from the Tony-winning Broadway sensation that every organist should know: All I Ask of You • Angel of Music • Masquerade • The Music of the Night • The Phantom of the Opera • The Point of No Return • Prima Donna • Think of Me • Wishing You Were Somehow Here Again.
00290300 $14.99

POP CLASSICS
24 FAVORITES ARRANGED FOR ORGAN
24 top hits, including: Can't Help Falling in Love • Daddy's Little Girl • Eleanor Rigby • Endless Love • Every Breath You Take • Hopelessly Devoted to You • Islands in the Stream • Let It Be • Mandy • Sea of Love • Unchained Melody • Woman in Love • Yesterday • You Needed Me • and more.
00199012 $9.95

SHOWTUNES
25 favorites from the stage to enjoy playing in your very own home! Includes: Bewitched • Blue Skies • Cabaret • Camelot • Edelweiss • Get Me to the Church on Time • Getting to Know You • I Could Write a Book • I Love Paris • Memory • Oklahoma • One • People • The Sound of Music • The Surrey with the Fringe on Top • Tomorrow • and more.
00199009 $9.95

SUNDAY SOLOS FOR ORGAN
PRELUDES, OFFERTORIES & POSTLUDES
Contains 30 blended selections perfect for organists to play every Sunday: Abide with Me • El Shaddai • He Is Exalted • Holy Ground • Lamb of Glory • A Mighty Fortress Is Our God • Rock of Ages • Via Dolorosa • What a Friend We Have in Jesus • and more.
00199016 $12.99

WONDERFUL STANDARDS
Take a trip down memory lane with these 25 gems arranged for organ: After You've Gone • Ain't Misbehavin' • Autumn Leaves • Bluesette • Body and Soul • Dinah • The Girl from Ipanema • How Deep Is the Ocean • How Insensitive • I Should Care • I've Got You Under My Skin • My Favorite Things • My Romance • Red Roses for a Blue Lady • September Song • So Nice (Summer Samba) • Watch What Happens • Younger Than Springtime • and more.
00199011 $9.95

HAL•LEONARD® CORPORATION
7777 W. BLUEMOUND RD. P.O. BOX 13819 MILWAUKEE, WI 53213

www.halleonard.com

Prices, contents, and availability subject to change without notice.

Christmas Collections

from Hal Leonard

All books arranged for piano, voice & guitar.

All-Time Christmas Favorites – Second Edition

This second edition features an all-star lineup of 32 Christmas classics, including: Blue Christmas • The Chipmunk Song • The Christmas Song • Frosty the Snow Man • Here Comes Santa Claus • I Saw Mommy Kissing Santa Claus • Jingle-Bell Rock • Let It Snow! Let It Snow! Let It Snow! • Merry Christmas, Darling • Nuttin' for Christmas • Rockin' Around the Christmas Tree • Rudolph the Red-Nosed Reindeer • Santa, Bring My Baby Back (To Me) • There Is No Christmas like a Home Christmas • and more.
00359051...$14.99

The Best Christmas Songs Ever – 6th Edition

69 all-time favorites are included in the 6th edition of this collection of Christmas tunes. Includes: Auld Lang Syne • Coventry Carol • Frosty the Snow Man • Happy Holiday • It Came Upon the Midnight Clear • O Holy Night • Rudolph the Red-Nosed Reindeer • Silver Bells • What Child Is This? • and many more.
00359130...$24.99

The Big Book of Christmas Songs – 2nd Edition

An outstanding collection of over 120 all-time Christmas favorites and hard-to-find classics. Features: Angels We Have Heard on High • As Each Happy Christmas • Auld Lang Syne • The Boar's Head Carol • Christ Was Born on Christmas Day • Bring a Torch Jeannette, Isabella • Carol of the Bells • Coventry Carol • Deck the Halls • The First Noel • The Friendly Beasts • God Rest Ye Merry Gentlemen • I Heard the Bells on Christmas Day • It Came Upon a Midnight Clear • Jesu, Joy of Man's Desiring • Joy to the World • Masters in This Hall • O Holy Night • The Story of the Shepherd • 'Twas the Night Before Christmas • What Child Is This? • and many more. Includes guitar chord frames.
00311520...$19.95

Christmas Songs – Budget Books

Save some money this Christmas with this fabulous budget-priced collection of 100 holiday favorites: All I Want for Christmas Is You • Christmas Time Is Here • Feliz Navidad • Grandma Got Run Over by a Reindeer • Happy Holiday • I'll Be Home for Christmas • Jesus Born on This Day • Last Christmas • Merry Christmas, Baby • O Holy Night • Please Come Home for Christmas • Rockin' Around the Christmas Tree • Some Children See Him • We Need a Little Christmas • What Child Is This? • and more.
00310887...$12.99

The Definitive Christmas Collection – 3rd Edition

Revised with even more Christmas classics, this must-have 3rd edition contains 127 top songs, such as: Blue Christmas • Christmas Time Is Here • Do You Hear What I Hear • The First Noel • A Holly Jolly Christmas • Jingle-Bell Rock • Little Saint Nick • Merry Christmas, Darling • O Holy Night • Rudolph, the Red-Nosed Reindeer • Silver and Gold • We Need a Little Christmas • You're All I Want for Christmas • and more!
00311602...$24.95

Essential Songs – Christmas

Over 100 essential holiday favorites: Blue Christmas • The Christmas Song • Deck the Hall • Frosty the Snow Man • A Holly Jolly Christmas • I'll Be Home for Christmas • Joy to the World • Let It Snow! Let It Snow! Let It Snow! • My Favorite Things • Rudolph the Red-Nosed Reindeer • Silver Bells • and more!
00311241...$24.95

The Muppet Christmas Carol

Matching folio to the blockbuster movie featuring 11 Muppet carols and eight pages of color photos. Bless Us All • Chairman of the Board • Christmas Scat • Finale - When Love Is Found/It Feels like Christmas • It Feels like Christmas • Marley and Marley • One More Sleep 'Til Christmas • Room in Your Heart • Scrooge • Thankful Heart • When Love Is Gone.
00312483...$14.95

Tim Burton's The Nightmare Before Christmas

This book features 11 songs from Tim Burton's creepy animated classic, with music and lyrics by Danny Elfman. Songs include: Jack's Lament • Jack's Obsession • Kidnap the Sandy Claws • Making Christmas • Oogie Boogie's Song • Poor Jack • Sally's Song • This Is Halloween • Town Meeting Song • What's This? • Finale/Reprise.
00312488...$12.99

Ultimate Christmas – 3rd Edition

100 seasonal favorites: Auld Lang Syne • Bring a Torch, Jeannette, Isabella • Carol of the Bells • The Chipmunk Song • Christmas Time Is Here • The First Noel • Frosty the Snow Man • Gesù Bambino • Happy Holiday • Happy Xmas (War Is Over) • Hymne • Jesu, Joy of Man's Desiring • Jingle-Bell Rock • March of the Toys • My Favorite Things • The Night Before Christmas Song • Pretty Paper • Silver and Gold • Silver Bells • Suzy Snowflake • What Child Is This • The Wonderful World of Christmas • and more.
00361399 ....$19.95